BRITAIN'S LIVING PAST

CONWAY
Bloomsbury Publishing Plc
50 Bedford Square, London,
WC1B 3DP, UK

BLOOMSBURY, CONWAY and the Conway logo
are trademarks of Bloomsbury Publishing Plc

First published in Great Britain 2019

A catalogue record for this book is available
from the British Library

Library of Congress Cataloguing-in-Publication
data has been applied for

ISBN: HB: 978-1-8448-6544-4
         ePub: 978-1-8448-6545-1
         ePDF: 978-1-8448-6542-0

2 4 6 8 10 9 7 5 3 1

Designed by Austin Taylor
Typeset in Source Sans Pro
Printed and bound in China by
C&C Offset Printing Co

Bloomsbury Publishing Plc makes every effort to
ensure that the papers used in the manufacture
of our books are natural, recyclable products
made from wood grown in well-managed forests.
Our manufacturing processes conform to the
environmental regulations of the country of origin.

To find out more about our authors and books
visit www.bloomsbury.com and sign up for our
newsletters

BRITAIN'S LIVING PAST

A Celebration of Britain's Surviving Traditional Cultural and Working Practices

WORDS *by* Anthony Burton

PHOTOGRAPHS *by* Rob Scott

CONWAY

LONDON · OXFORD · NEW YORK · NEW DELHI · SYDNEY

CONTENTS

INTRODUCTION

There was a time, not so very long ago, when history seemed to consist entirely of kings and queens, famous battles and Acts of Parliament. But there has always been another history, the history of the everyday life of the people, and it can be expressed in many different forms.

There are the industries and crafts that continue to produce all kinds of goods and materials using techniques that, in many cases, have scarcely changed for centuries. At the opposite extreme are the things we do in our spare time, our games and sports – and some have survived unchanged for a very long time indeed. It is this sense of continuity that we have tried to capture in the subjects chosen for this book.

The range is wide, and even so the choice has not always been easy. There were far more subjects that could have been included, but we have tried to select ones that each shed a different light on the past – as well as those that we both found to be intrinsically interesting. After all, if the writer and photographer are bored, why should you, the reader, have any interest in their book? It has sometimes been a journey of discovery for both of us – neither of us, for example, were quite prepared for the mayhem that is the Ashbourne football match. Some subjects were old favourites for one or other of us – Anthony has long been an enthusiastic participant in barge matches, while Rob has known Swaledale for many years. But one overriding rule covered everything: for every site or activity we covered, there had to be a real sense that it was still around because it still served a real need or because it was part of a tradition that no one wanted to see simply die away. There had to be a real feeling that what we were seeing was a real, living tradition, continuing to this day because it had an intrinsic value. It is always a thrill to feel that sense of continuity, and we hope that we have managed to recreate something of the same sensation in the following pages.

A
MARITIME
NATION

THE SHIPWRIGHT

In this book we are looking at heritage and tradition in many different forms, but there is no tradition that has done more to shape the history of these islands than its long maritime past. This is a heritage that stretches back far beyond written records.

The earliest sailing craft that consisted of anything more than hollowed-out logs were found in the mud of the Humber at North Ferriby, and dating techniques showed them to have been built in around 1500 BC. Over the centuries, vessels were developed and became ever more sophisticated, with the larger ships carrying a vast spread of sail on many masts. These were the vessels that could trade around the world, culminating in the famous fast clipper ships, such as *Cutty Sark*, that were originally built to bring tea from China. This was a luxury commodity, and the first load to be brought home always fetched the highest price – hence the emphasis on speed. But there was also a fascinating array of smaller vessels that never left home waters, trading around the coast. Each region had its own speciality, ranging from the square-rigged Humber keel – the nearest thing we now have to a medieval ship – to more elaborate topsail schooners. But one thing they all have in common is that they were built out of wood by shipwrights.

In our search for a traditional shipwright still working on wooden boats, one of the criteria we chose was that ideally the work would be done in a building that itself had some historic significance. That requirement was met in a way that hardly seemed possible. Stirling & Son work in what might well be the most historically significant surviving dockyard building in Britain: No. 1 Slip at the former Royal Naval Dockyard at Devonport.

When William of Orange came to the throne as William III, one of his early demands was for a brand-new naval dockyard to be created at Plymouth. Work began in 1690 and the original site eventually became the South Yard, mainly developed in the 18th century. Among the new structures was No. 1 Slip, on which work began in the 1770s. It was here that a number of famous warships were built.

← Will Stirling at work on the 'gentleman's cutter' *Integrity*.

→ Applying protective copper sheathing to the hull of *Integrity*.

PREVIOUS PAGES
The magnificent covered slipway at Plymouth dockyard, built in 1814.

But building in the open air creates difficulties, with work often held up by bad weather. So in 1814 it was roofed over and has remained substantially the same ever since. It is the oldest surviving covered slip of any British naval yard, and as a major historical monument it is a listed building. Its rating is the same as that given to Stonehenge, for example, which gives a good idea of just how important it is. And it is in this building that Will Stirling and his men build and repair wooden vessels of up to 200 tons.

The building looks interesting enough as you get nearer to it, but it's only when you step inside that the full majesty of the structure becomes apparent – as well as its complexity. The original slip was built up against the tall stone dockyard wall, which now forms one side of the structure. The opposite side of the slipway is a slatted wooden wall that turns inward towards the two ends, which are both entirely open.

The structure was designed by Sir Robert Seppings, a distinguished naval architect who made significant advances in the design of hulls of wooden vessels. The roof itself, with its sheet-metal covering, is extraordinarily complex, with cantilevered rafters, angled braces and horizontal collars. It is perhaps not too fanciful to imagine the whole roof taken off and turned upside down on the ground, at which point it might be mistaken for a rather odd ship's hull. It doesn't seem to matter how many times you come here, it still takes the breath away, and anyone who, like myself, is not a qualified architect can only wonder at how such a thing could ever have been devised.

In the 21st century much of the work that had been carried out by the navy was privatised, and a large part of the complex became available for private companies – and that included the South Yard and No. 1 Slip – so that is when Will Stirling took over

the lease. It was only later that he discovered there was already a family connection. One of his ancestors had married an admiral, and in 1798 she was given the honour of launching HMS *Foudroyant* from this very slip shortly after it had been completed. In 1800 *Foudroyant* became the flagship of a comparatively young rear admiral – Horatio Nelson. So Will's connection with the site goes back almost to the day the slip was first built. But his own route into boatbuilding was far from direct.

At the age of 19, Will, already an enthusiastic sailor, bought a 19ft boat, built in 1938, and set about restoring it. It led to a passion for boatbuilding, and he went to college to study the subject. At the end of his studies, he took the engineless 19-footer and sailed her to Norway, returning via the north coast of Scotland and ending the voyage in Cornwall. Here he got an apprenticeship with a Cornish company that specialised in

building pilot cutters. As working vessels, the essential feature of these crafts was speed. The pilot's job was to guide a larger ship safely into harbour – and there were usually more pilots than ships requiring help, so it was a case of the first one on board getting the job.

With his training and experience, Will embarked on building his first wooden vessel, a replica of an 1835 smuggler's lugger. He sailed her over to Iceland, came back and sold her, and used the money to set up in business as a builder and restorer of wooden boats. His next major undertaking was a replica of a gentleman's cutter, a popular

design of yacht for the wealthy, based on the well-tested design of the old pilot cutters. Will designed her and built her with his team in 2012. In 2017 she was back on the slip, being prepared for a big adventure: she was due to sail to the Arctic to go through the Northwest Passage. But before work on her or any other vessel could begin, Will had to get the slip itself into a usable condition after some 60 years of neglect.

....
↓ The winch used to haul vessels up and down the slipway.

....
OVERLEAF Restoration work under way on a 160-ton vessel from Norway.

To do so would require a lot of work, and fortunately a grant was available. So rails were put in place on the slip and a winch acquired from the RNLI. These are essentials if vessels are to be brought in for work and relaunched when the work is completed. There are two tracks, each of which carries a substantial wheeled metal cradle that can be moved up and down the rails, powered by the winch. A vessel can arrive at the foot of the slip at high tide, when it can be floated over the cradle. As the tide retreats, the vessel settles down onto the cradle, where it is secured and can then be hauled up above

the high-tide mark. The process is reversed when it is time to go, the vessel being lowered and floated off.

As I walked into Will's decidedly spartan office, the first thing that caught my eye was a caulking hammer. When you are hoping to find someone who really is using traditional methods, it is an encouraging start to find this fundamental tool of wooden shipbuilding. No matter how well constructed a wooden hull might be, it still has to be treated to make it perfectly watertight. The seams are caulked by pushing a fibrous material between the planks. In the bad old days, oakum was produced by convicts unravelling old rope. That may not be how it is produced these days, but the technique is the same: the caulking tool has a triangular blade that is used to force the material home by hitting it with the caulking hammer. Caulking in one form or another goes back to the earliest wooden boats to take to the water.

Another old technique was in progress on the slip where the cutter *Integrity* was being prepared for her voyage through the Northwest Passage. A problem that beset older wooden vessels on long voyages was that various marine creatures would make their home on the hull beneath the waterline, among them the marine worm that had the unfortunate habit of boring holes in the planking. The answer developed during the 18th century was to cover the affected area with thin copper sheeting. And that is precisely what was being done here. It's a fairly straightforward business along the sides, but where there are awkward shapes, such as around the rudder, a template has to be made first and then the copper cut to fit. And, of course, when you have to cover the bottom of the hull, fixing the sheets while lying flat on your back is not the most comfortable job to undertake.

The *Integrity* is a truly beautiful, elegant craft and, like all cutters, designed to carry a lot of sail for whenever it might be needed. Altogether there are 2,000 square feet available, and her rigging is suitably versatile. The mast can be extended upwards to carry a topsail, and an extra spar can be set up to carry a square sail for running before the wind. As one might expect from a 'gentleman's cutter', the carpentry is all carried out to perfection, and this is a feature of the yard. Everyone is expected to be able to turn their hand to anything: the contract with the work force ends with the catch-all phrase 'and any other shipyard duties that might be required'. So you might find yourself working at the very delicate job of applying decorative gold leaf to the hull in the morning – a job where even small mistakes can prove very expensive – and then bashing out hefty keel bolts in the afternoon. Inevitably, some are better at certain jobs than others, perhaps more skilled at joinery, and they will get the jobs where their particular skills are needed. And a new generation is being trained to follow on – Will currently has two apprentices at work.

Work was also under way on a second boat, a 160-ton Norwegian vessel that required a good deal of work, including replacing planking on the hull. There is a special problem associated with this work, which is that a ship's hull does not consist of convenient straight lines, but instead curves in at bow and stern. So the question is how do you fix a 3-inch-thick wooden plank to a curved section? The answer is that you heat it up in a special steam chest and then, once it has become flexible, it is quickly brought into place and clamped in position, ready to be permanently fixed. This is a job requiring five strong workers.

Will also has his own line in clinker-built sailing dinghies. Clinker construction again takes us back to the very earliest days of sail – perhaps the most famous examples of early clinker-built vessels were the Viking longships. Instead of the planks being nailed to the hull to present a smooth surface as on the Norwegian vessel, they overlap each other. The yard has standard patterns for creating the hull shape, so although it is hardly mass production, it can turn out a string of identical dinghies. There was one in the yard when I visited, and what is striking is that the finish is every bit as fine as it is on the grander yacht. It has a simple lugsail, and it is the sort of vessel that it is really good fun to muck about in, and remarkably seaworthy despite its size.

This is a yard where quality is everything. Will never pays for advertising, but relies entirely on recommendations from his very satisfied customers. It is an attitude that permeates the whole workforce – everyone knows that getting the next job depends on doing the one in hand to the very highest possible standard. I talked about tradition in the introduction, and the whole idea of tradition was reinforced when Will mentioned the next vessel due in for restoration. She was built at the Scott and Linton yard at Dumbarton on the Clyde – the yard that launched one of Britain's most famous sailing ships, the *Cutty Sark*. If the workforce from that yard where she was built in 1869 came down to this dock at Plymouth today, they could probably start work tomorrow with very little further training. And they would certainly recognise the same quality of craftsmanship as had been expected from them a century and a half ago.

THE ROPE WORKS

Building a sailing ship is one thing, but it also had to be rigged, and that involved working with an enormous quantity of rope. Master ropemakers are based at the historic dockyard of Chatham, which certainly earns the name 'historic' as it was established here in 1547, soon becoming the most important dockyard in the kingdom.

A good measure of just how important it was can be gauged from the wage bills for this and the other naval yards for 1584, when Chatham paid out £3,680 and the next highest was Deptford at £205, while Portsmouth lagged far behind at a mere £30. And in all that time the yard was making rope, because sailing ships created a huge demand. The most famous ship ever built at Chatham has to be Nelson's flagship *Victory*, which, it is said, had between 26 and 27 miles of rigging. And producing the rope needed for the maiden voyage would not have been the end of the matter: rope made of natural fibres rots with time and heavy usage, so a lot more replacement rope would have been needed. The ropemakers of Chatham would never have been short of work – and they still make rope here today, even though the Royal Navy no longer has a presence. But although the principles of rope-making have never changed, technology has, not surprisingly, advanced since the 16th century.

Originally, rope was made from natural fibres, particularly hemp, and the whole process was done by hand. To simplify the process: fibres are attached to hooks on a wheel and the bulk of the fibres are wound round the ropemaker's waist. As the ropemaker walks away from the wheel, paying out the fibres, a boy turns the wheel so that the fibres are twisted together. To get a usable length of rope entailed a long walk back – hence the term 'ropewalk' is still used to this day, even when machines have taken over. That mechanisation did not happen at Chatham until 1811, when the great engineer Henry Maudsley introduced his forming machine. Incredibly, that original machine not only still exists but is still in use at Chatham, doing exactly the same job it was built to do, though on our visit the main work was being carried out by a more recent machine, built here in 1856.

Arriving at Chatham on a dank, grey morning in January when the mist seemed to blot out all signs of modern life was like stepping into a 19th-century world of gaunt industrial buildings. The rope-making originally took place in two parallel buildings, separated by a cobbled alleyway. On one side was the spinning complex, where the raw material was turned into thread, and where a notice still announces 'Women Spinners Only'. Opposite that is the ropewalk itself, built in 1785, traditionally a male bastion, though there is now the very first female

ropemaker here. Stepping inside, one finds an amazing space: rows of windows to either side, but otherwise just one immensely long structure with the far end so far away that it's all but invisible. When it was being built the Admiralty had come to an important decision: the British fleet must be able to anchor anywhere in the world, so each ship had

to carry a sufficient length of anchor cable to make this possible (this was in the days before iron chains were used). It was decided that the maximum depth should be 40 fathoms (240 feet to landlubbers), for which they would require 120 fathoms of cable. Making allowance for the space needed at both ends of the building and the fact that the rope reduces in length slightly during the making process, it was decided that the ideal length for the new building would be 440 yards – that is, a quarter of a mile. It's no wonder that these days you see bikes propped up all over the place for the workers to make a quick run from one end to the other.

↓ Pulling off the rope from the capstan used to haul the carriage down the rope walk.

PREVIOUS PAGES
Looking down the quarter-mile-long rope walk at Chatham dockyard – the carriage has rotating hooks that twist the strands to create rope.

Mechanisation reversed the process used in the old days. Originally, the man with the yarn walked away from the rotating hooks to twist them together. Now it is the rotating plate with the hooks that is moved, using a wheeled carriage. The start of the process was at the very far end of the walk. The spun fibre, in this case coir from coconuts, arrives wound on to bobbins known as cops that are then arranged on a frame. The individual threads are then fed through holes in a circular plate to keep them separate, the whole setup looking very similar to the traditional warping frame in a weaving mill. The threads are then drawn through a metal tube to form what may look like a rope, but it has no strength because none of the yarn threads have yet been twisted together. The untwisted threads are pulled out of the tube and fastened to one of the hooks on the travelling carriage, the forming machine. This can now be hauled back down the ropewalk by a rope running from a capstan at the far end of the building, where a second worker puts a couple of twists round the large pulley

↑ Attaching the twisted strands to the moveable carriage.

↑ With a workplace 440 yards long, bikes make it easier to get about.

at the side of the machine. Originally the capstan would have been worked by hand, and later by a steam engine, but it is now powered by electricity. As the carriage begins to move, gearing from the axle sets the plate with the hooks spinning round. The third team member has the job of steering the forming machine on its long, slow journey.

It is impossible for the three workers to communicate with each other – even with the lungs of Pavarotti, no one could make themselves heard over such a long distance. Instead there are bells at each end, worked by a simple string pull. A bell tells the man on the capstan that everything's ready to move and he can start the motor. If the bell rings again, that's a message to stop. This happens at regular intervals, as the coir strands are not very strong and are liable to break, so there has to be a pause while the broken ends are located and knotted together again.

Rope-making is not a job for the impatient. As it progresses down the walk, supports are put in at regular intervals to stop the rope sagging. Once it has reached the end of its long journey and that strand is complete it is cut at the standing end, and it is only then that you become aware of the tension in the rope that whips away at speed (fortunately the cutter knows from experience which way it's going to fly). It is then hooked up at the far end and tied in place.

This is not yet a complete rope, it is just one strand. The rope being made that day would consist of three strands altogether, so this whole operation has to be repeated again and then again. Now the final stage is reached when the rope is closed by twisting the three strands together, so there is yet one more journey to be made. In the past, the rope would have had a coloured thread down the centre, the 'rogue's thread'. Each dockyard had its own colour, so any rope could be identified. If there was a bad batch, then everyone knew who had made it – and if Chatham housewives suddenly sported

some remarkably new, clean washing lines, a simple check would discover whether they had been acquired legally. In today's rope there is one break with tradition: measurements have gone metric and the rope being made that day was 64mm in diameter. The old admirals would surely have been horrified to find their ropes being made to a measurement devised by their arch enemy, the French!

The company no longer makes rope for the Navy, but it still operates in exactly the same way it did more than a century ago, and there is a demand for traditional ropework for rigging on historic ships. Some famous names have been supplied, including the *Cutty Sark* and the *Victory*, but visitors to Chatham don't have to go that far to see ropes made here. All they have to do is visit the *Gannet*, a Victorian sloop that now has a permanent home in the nearby dry dock.

This is real tradition at work, with historic machines still doing what they were built to do and surviving in the commercial world, providing ropes of many different sizes and using many different materials, from manila to synthetic fibres. The company makes ropes for its own stock to sell on a retail basis, and also to specific requirements for customers. But if a Victorian ropemaker came back today, he would be able to start work straight away – and if he came in winter he'd find it just as freezingly cold as he remembered it being in his own time. More importantly, he'd recognise that the quality of the rope being turned out today would have been just as acceptable to any working sailor as it would have been before the age of steam made the sailing ship obsolete.

PREVIOUS PAGES
Individual strands are wound onto bobbins and passed to a perforated circular plate for alignment *(left)*.

Drawing strands through a tube attached to the circular plate – they will be twisted together to form rope *(right)*.

→ Starting the process of forming a rope.

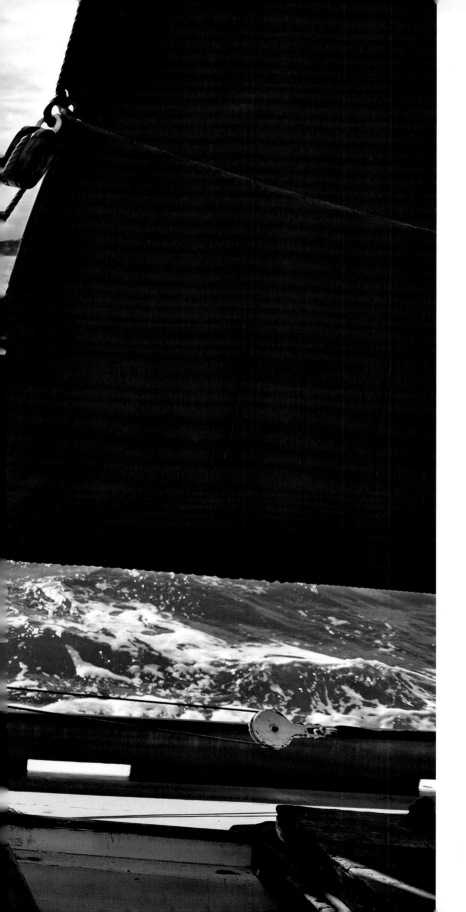

THE BARGE
MATCH

The largest vessels out of all the rich variety of coastal traders that were worked with a two-man crew were the Thames barges. The name is slightly misleading as these craft actually traded all round the south-east coast of England and well up into East Anglia.

They developed into their present form over many years. They had their origins in the 'dumb' barges and lighters on the Thames that moved with the tide and were used for loading and unloading cargo ships. Over the years they developed shaped hulls, with finer lines and overhanging bows and sterns – rather like oversized punts. In time a short mast with a single sail was added, and the lighters became sailing barges. Their distinctive feature that makes them instantly recognisable today, the spritsail, arrived from the Netherlands at the end of the 17th century. These Dutch vessels still carried square sails, but instead of being set from a yardarm at right angles to the hull, the sail was set fore and aft, and its peak, the top corner furthest from the mast, was extended by the sprit, a spar running at an angle from the foot of the mast. On Thames barges, the sail is controlled by sheets, with the ropes running from the clew, the lower aft corner of the sail. This line is attached to a block system that can slide along a horizontal bar, the horse. When tacking, the block moves from one end of the horse to the other, as the wind catches the opposite side of the sail. The peak is controlled through separate lines running down to the deck, known as the vangs – pronounced 'wangs'.

The spritsail barge was an immediate success, and it was to develop even further over the years. A topsail was added above the mainsail; a mizzen sail was added on a short mast in the stern; and foresails were attached in front of the main mast. In the largest vessels, a bowsprit was added, allowing extra triangular jib sails to be attached. As barges became bigger, handling them by means of a tiller became more difficult, and the steering wheel was introduced.

These vessels were vital to the development of south-east England, and of London in particular. In the great housing boom of the 19th century, vast quantities of bricks were delivered by barge; and before the age of the motor vehicle, when people's main form of transport was horse-drawn carriage, London depended on stack barges to bring in hay and straw needed for the huge number of horses stabled in the capital. Another feature of the Thames barge that was necessary when the vessel had to go round the coast rather than stay in rivers and creeks was the keel, which stabilised seagoing vessels, preventing them from skittering about in the wind. But a deep keel would have made the use of barges in shallower creeks impossible, greatly reducing their value. So lee boards were introduced. These are heavy wooden structures, either triangular or pear shaped, one to each side of the vessel. As the name suggests, when the wind is blowing to one side of the vessel, a board is dropped into the water on the other, the lee side. It is

an efficient system, but requires a certain amount of hard work from the crew member. Dropping the board down is simple enough, but winching it back up again is altogether more exacting.

Working the boat efficiently takes skill and experience. The skipper generally takes the helm, as it is vital to know the complex channels of the estuaries in which the boat is sailing and to be able to assess the wind and tide to make the most efficient passage possible – when working a barge, time really is money. The skipper got paid by the load, not according to how long it took him to reach port. The job of the second crew member is to control the movement

of the different sails every time the vessel comes about when tacking, and to raise and lower the appropriate lee boards. Trading barges kept going well into the second half of the 20th century, but with increasing competition there were desperate attempts to cut costs. I sailed with a former barge skipper some years ago, and at the end of the trading era he was working his vessel singlehanded. It must have made for an extraordinarily hard life.

A large number of Thames barges have survived to today, still trading in a sense, in that many of them are used for charter work, instead of carrying cargo, with their holds converted into living accommodation. One tradition has, however, survived completely intact – the barge match. In 1863 a gentleman called Henry Dodd initiated a contest for Thames barges to race against each other. It was not organised as a fun event: the idea was to see which barges gave the best performance and to identify the features that had helped them win. The object was to improve performance, but, of course, there were limiting factors. If speed was the only consideration, then a sleek yacht would outpace any barge, but it would have no room for cargo. So what was being sought was the perfect combination of good performance and large carrying capacity, always keeping in mind that crew must still be limited to two. Barge enthusiasts tell a story that may or may not be true, but everyone hopes it is: the problem of producing such a vessel was set as a computer exercise – and the perfect design proved, of course, to be a typical spritsail barge. For those of us with a love of traditional sail there is no finer sight than a whole fleet of barges competing in a match, of which many are held each year around Britain's south-east coast.

....

↓ Today Thames barges are used for pleasure and holds have been converted into living accommodation – the saloon on *Mirosa*.

PREVIOUS PAGES Setting sail on *Mirosa* at the start of the Thames Barge match.

→ Going aloft to set the topsail.

OVERLEAF
The barge *Marjorie* looking magnificent with all sails set *(left)*.

Skipper Peter Dodds out on the bowsprit setting a jib sail *(right)*.

PS *WAVERLEY*

The paddle steamer *Waverley* is the only remaining seagoing paddle steamer at work anywhere in the world. She represents a long tradition that saw the citizens of Glasgow going 'doon th'water' – taking steamer excursions down the Clyde to enjoy the fresh air of Scotland's west coast.

The very first commercial paddle steamer, *Comet*, went into service right back in 1812, having been ordered by Henry Bell, a hotelier in Helensburgh, from where she plied the waters of the Clyde and took trips round the coast until she foundered on Craignish Point in 1820. She was very different from today's steamers, with no deck and all her passengers in the open – and basking in the reassurance that if the new-fangled steam engine failed, then sail could take over. The large square sail hung from a spar fastened to the top of the tall funnel. PS *Comet* might be considered crude by modern standards, but she was a success with the public, and soon other entrepreneurs were recognising that there was a ready market for passengers wishing to escape the smoke and grime of the busy industrial city. Steamer piers were built on the islands and up the sea lochs of the west coast, and new resorts such as Rothesay on Bute and Brodick on Arran flourished.

These early steamers offered more than just an excursion out on the water: without exception they had music on board. It could be quite grand – the *Duchess of York*, for example, offered passengers a concert by the Berliner Philharmonisches Blas-Orchester – but one suspects that others provided less august entertainment. A reporter from the *Glasgow Herald* took a steamer trip in 1888, and what he found might have been more typical: 'A penny brass whistle and a cracked violin.' One of the most popular writers of the 19th century was Sir Walter Scott, and his Waverley novels were particular favourites, so it is no surprise to find Clyde steamers carrying the name. The year 1899 saw the launch of *Waverley III*, which remained in service right up to 1940, when she joined the flotilla of vessels going to Dunkirk. She did not survive.

Many of the Scottish paddle steamers were run by railway companies, starting with the North British in 1865. In 1947 the London

← The magnificent
triple-expansion
steam engine is a
great attraction for
passengers.

PREVIOUS PAGES
The paddle steamer
Waverley alongside the
jetty at Gairloch Pier.

& North Eastern Railway ordered the fourth *Waverley* from the Clyde shipbuilders A & J Inglis. She worked the popular excursion route from the Clyde near Helensburgh round the coast and up Loch Long to Arrochar.

By the 1970s, paddle-steamer excursions had lost some of their popularity and the *Waverley* was starting to show her age. She was withdrawn from service and looked likely to follow many other paddle steamers to the breakers' yard. But instead she was bought by the Paddle Steamer Preservation Society, restored and returned to the water. Today, she no longer limits her trips to a single journey, and though her home port remains Glasgow, she now makes journeys right along the British coast from the Hebrides to the Thames in London.

One look at the *Waverley* and it's clear why she was worth preserving. This is a handsome vessel, with her two funnels, her smart livery in red, white and black, her fine lines and her shapely paddle boxes. She looks the way ships used to look, unlike, for example, so many modern liners and cruise ships that resemble floating blocks of flats. This is a slender vessel, 235 feet long and just 30 feet across the beam, and although she has a theoretical top speed of 18.5 knots, nowadays she keeps to a more sedate 13 knots, as befits a lady past her 70th birthday. On board, there is nothing to take away from that first impression, from the varnished wooden benches on deck to the saloons and bars down below. It is a pleasure to be a passenger, with the promise of a trip to take in some of Britain's finest coastal scenery.

↓ The paddle boxes to either side of the hull give paddle steamers their unique profile.

↗ *Waverley* under way off Scotland's west coast.

If that were all that was available it would be sufficient to ensure a thoroughly enjoyable day out, but the *Waverley* has something very special to offer in addition.

In the middle of the 19th century Captain James Wilkinson of the Caledonian Company noticed that many people seemed curious about the machinery that drove the vessel along. He thought that they might enjoy actually being able to see the engine at work, so a Clyde steamer was built that had a walkway along one side of the engine room. His hunch proved to be absolutely right: the passengers loved it, and soon all Clyde steamers had open engine rooms – and the *Waverley* is no exception. You don't have to be a steam buff or even know anything about mechanics to be fascinated by the sight. She is powered by a mighty triple-expansion engine. Put simply, steam at high pressure is passed into a 24-inch-diameter cylinder, where it expands, pushing the piston along. But now, instead of simply being allowed to drift away, because it is still under considerable pressure the steam is passed on to a second cylinder. This has to be larger (and is in fact 39 inches across) to take account of the reduced pressure, but once

again the steam expands and pushes the piston along, and there is still enough of it left for it to work a third time in the last, biggest low-pressure cylinder, measuring 62 inches in diameter. Working together, these cylinders produce an impressive 2,100 horsepower. But you don't need to know any of that to enjoy the spectacle of these massive chunks of metal on the move, as the pistons go in and out with a gentle swish and hiss, and the connecting rods turn the great shaft that passes out at either side to the paddles. I have to confess to being slightly prejudiced, being more than enchanted by steam

↑ Inside the wheelhouse.

engines, but there is nothing quite like the engine room of the *Waverley*. For once, that often-misused word *unique* really does apply.

A wide range of excursions is available throughout the summer, including even a trip to Northern Ireland, but there is still something special about the Scottish trips. This is the work she was built for, and these journeys take in the river that has seen some of Britain's finest and best-loved ships being built, even though those days have largely gone. There is a certain sense of sadness

in cruising down the Clyde in Glasgow and passing the enormous Titan crane towering over what was once the famous John Brown shipyard where such iconic vessels as the *Queen Mary* were built. Today the crane is virtually all that remains of that glorious past. But there is still the same sense of excitement about leaving a city by water to arrive in the very different environment of the Highlands and Islands of the west coast. To travel on the *Waverley* is more than just having an enjoyable day out – it is to participate in this country's great maritime heritage. Long may she steam.

← *Waverley* travels round the British coast and here she makes a spectacular entrance into London, passing under Tower Bridge.

ON THE MOVE

THE WHEELWRIGHT AND COACH BUILDER

On the edge of Colyton in Devon, close by the church and a green, there is a slightly ramshackle collection of single-storey buildings that could house almost any process, but the clues as to its actual use are there in plenty.

A newly painted wagon stands outside and a number of wooden wheels are propped against walls. These are the workshops of Mike Rowland and Son, wheelwrights and carriage builders. It was Mike Rowland who started the business half a century ago, and he taught his son Greg. Mike is now in his seventies but seems to have no interest in retirement, and their success can be gauged by the sign over the door announcing they have a royal warrant. What exactly do they do for the royal family? However much they might like to, that is something they can never discuss, or the warrant would be forfeited. But possessing such a warrant is itself a mark of their fine craftsmanship – though that is not a word Greg is very fond of. His is not a craft, he declares, but a trade. He feels, probably rightly, that the word 'craft' has, in recent times, been associated with a certain degree of amateurism, and they are complete professionals. But talking to Greg and watching him at work with his father and their young journeyman, George Richards, it is clear that craftsmanship, in its truest sense, is exactly what one is seeing.

   A quick tour provided a taste of the amazing variety of work on hand. The brightly coloured wagon looked magnificent in the sunshine, but Greg was quite dismissive of it – it was all wrong, apparently, with the body not appropriate to the frame. Inside was a huge pantechnicon and a Somerset Levels cart. The latter is not to be confused with a Somerset cart. As anyone who has travelled around the rural areas of the county will know, this is a landscape of narrow

lanes, and Somerset carts are appropriately narrow to deal with them. But out on the Levels, there is no such problem, and this cart from Westonzoyland is huge, and will need quite a lot of restoration to the body as well as a new set of wheels. More unusual is a horse-drawn omnibus, and that too will need completely new wheels. Completing the set are cannon, Greg's favourites, partly because of his own military background, but also because, once they are completed with new wheels, these particular cannon will have a home in the magnificent setting of the Chelsea Hospital in London. Lots of jobs, each requiring something different, but in essence the making of a wooden wheel remains much as it has done for centuries – even if machines have taken over a few aspects of the work.

There are four main parts to a wooden wheel: the hub, the spokes and the rim, all made of wood (though a cannon wheel is rather different as it has a metal hub), and the metal tyre. Traditionally, the hub was made of elm, because its twisted grain is particularly dense, but following the devastation caused by Dutch elm disease, mature elm has been extremely scarce and alternatives have to be found. The wheelwright is always having to make judgements over which wood is appropriate for which job, as Greg explained. The standard work on the wheelwright was written in the 19th century and later wheelwrights tended to take it as being the final word on the subject. In it, the only wood mentioned for wheels was elm, and that was because that was the wood the author happened to use in his part of the world –

but Greg has found old wheels made from a variety of different timbers, even one made of Douglas fir that had survived for many years. So he has felt free to make his own choices. One traditional material has been mahogany, but that is no longer a sustainable resource, so he has moved to sapele, a member of the same family, also known as African mahogany. In other cases he might use oak and ash. It all comes down to that invaluable commodity – experience.

The hub is marked out and trimmed with a bandsaw before being turned on a lathe. The spokes will be fitted in using mortise and tenon joints, but that is not as simple as it might sound as the spokes are dished, moving slightly outward, so the mortise has to be cut into the hub at an angle – and, of course, each mortise has to be at precisely the same angle. And it all has to be done very accurately, for no glue is ever used in a wheel. The spokes themselves are first roughed out on a copying lathe. This is not exactly introducing modern technology, as the machine was invented two centuries ago by Thomas Blanchard, who worked in the great centre of firearm manufacturing, Springfield, Massachusetts. He recognised that the butts of rifles and muskets were all exactly the same shape when they came from the factory, and thought that it should be possible to duplicate that shape using a standard model. And basically, the copying lathe here does exactly the same job. For the spokes that were being made, Greg had only needed to make one spoke by hand, and that would be the pattern for all the subsequent spokes for that set of wheels. This spoke was placed in the centre of the lathe, with two other pieces of timber to either side that would be cut to exactly the same shape. Once the machine is set in motion, a follower runs over the surface of the pattern, and the

→ Welding a metal strip to form a circular tyre.

← Mike Rowland using a traditional spoke-shave to give shape to a wheel.

PREVIOUS PAGES
Shrinking a metal tyre onto a wooden wheel at Mike Rowland & Son's workshops at Colyton, Devon.

cutters above the other four spokes are then given precisely the same motion. It would take Greg about half an hour to make a spoke by hand – but now these four spokes are ready in just eight minutes.

At this stage, the spokes are still only roughed out; they will be finished by hand, and here the technology has not changed for centuries. The wheelwright sits on a spoke horse, a bench with a foot treadle to which the spoke can be clamped and then given its exact shape using a spokeshave, a simple device with the cutting blade held centrally between the two handles. Once completed, the spokes have to be fitted into the hub – tightly but not too tight. Everything will be tightened up during the final part of the process. Once again, knowing just how tight comes down to the sort of judgement that only comes with experience, which is why George only got his journeyman status after a long apprenticeship.

The outer rim consists of segments known here as fellies, in other parts as felloes. These can be accurately shaped using templates, a selection of which hang

on the workshop wall. They are joined together using dowels, and mortises are cut to allow the ends of the spokes to be attached. When the whole wooden wheel is assembled, the joints are not yet quite perfectly fitted. If the fellies butted hard against each other, then when the tyre was shrunk on, the process would end before the joints at the hub had been made tight. In wheelwright's language, they would be felly bound. The wheel still needs a lot of work to refine the details: the rim is chamfered with a slight curve to match the curve of the spokes, so that everything presents a harmonious whole. A great deal of planning, shaving and sanding goes on before the wooden parts are exactly as they should be.

The final stage is to fit the tyre. Originally this would have been made of wrought iron, but scarcely any of this is made these days, and mild steel is a perfectly adequate substitute. First the wheel has to be measured with a traveller, but that does not provide the final measurement – the fellies are still slightly apart, and that has to be compensated for. One aspect of the

wheelwright's skill lies in knowing exactly how closely the tyre must fit to pull everything together and make the whole wheel firm, without any movement of any of the joints. Once that measurement has been made, the steel strip is cut to the correct length and bent, and the two ends are welded together. Now comes the spectacular part.

Out in the courtyard is a circular metal tyre plate. The wheel is placed over the centre post and firmly clamped in position. A fire will already have been lit, and when it has reached a fierce heat, an old pallet is slung on top and the metal ring placed on top of that. Knowing when it is ready is a matter of careful judgement. What is absolutely certain is that it must not reach red heat as that could cause it to twist when lifted from the flames. The colour to look for is a gunmetal grey, and the carbon particles from the burning wood must be seen dancing off the surface. The ring is then picked up using tongs and quickly taken from the fire, and one helper holds it firmly in place while the ring is positioned over the wood with tyre dogs and tapped into place with hammers. It is essential that it is correctly positioned, with a slight lip, and the welded joint on the steel must not coincide with a joint between fellies. Then it is rapidly cooled with water before it has a chance to scorch the outside of the wheel. It all happens very quickly, and there is one last test – the finished metal rim is struck with a hammer. This is the test that used to be applied to locomotive wheels in the days of steam, and the critereria are the same. If it gives out a reverberating ringing sound, all is well; if it is no more than a dull thud, something has gone wrong. To no one's surprise, on this particular occasion the result was perfect. One of the hundred or so wheels that would be made here in the year was ready for painting, if needed, or for sending on to the client.

↑ Levering the tyre into place *(top)*. The completed wheel *(bottom)*.

→ Cooling the tyre to shrink it firmly to the rim of the wheel.

THE HORSE TRAM

People visit the Isle of Man for all kinds of reasons, but for anyone interested in the history of transport it offers something totally unique – three different transport systems, each of which is over a century old, and all of them running out of Douglas. Of the three, the horse tram is certainly the rarest and continues a tradition that goes back to the days when if you didn't want to use your own two feet to get about the country, you had to rely on the horse.

The system has its British origins in railed tracks for horse-drawn vehicles that were introduced at the beginning of the 17th century – but they were never intended for passengers and were mostly used to carry coal from inland mines to river banks for loading onto vessels. The early versions were rather crude with wooden rails, but later iron rails were introduced and 18th-century engineers conducted experiments to see how they compared with wagons on an ordinary road. The results were impressive: a single horse could haul two tons with a wagon on an ordinary road, but put that wagon onto an iron track and the load went up to an impressive eight tons. The iron-railed systems became known as tramways. It was on just such a tramway that the first experiments with steam locomotives were carried out, and by the 1830s passengers were being taken by steam along tracks linking towns and cities. But no one necessarily wanted steam locomotives puffing down their streets and throwing out clouds of sooty smoke – and certainly not in a seaside town that prided itself on its fresh, healthy sea air. So if a new railed track was going to be supplied for holidaymakers, it made sense to go back to the old ways – namely, tramcars drawn by horses.

By the 1870s the Isle of Man had a booming tourist trade and in Douglas the old complex of streets and modest housing was cleared away to develop the town into a fashionable seaside resort, with a promenade stretching almost the full length of the bay. Now all that was needed was a suitable transport system. Thomas Lightfoot from Lancashire had worked on a number of railway projects and in 1873 had built a horse tramway for Sheffield Corporation. On visiting the Isle of Man, he decided that such a system would be ideal for Douglas. He managed to get permission for the plan and in 1876 the Douglas Bay Tramway was born. The track was laid along the length of the bay for just over a mile and a half, from the pier at the south to the point where the land begins to rise up to Onchan Head. Initially just a single track was laid, with rails 3 feet apart, which became the standard gauge for the island's later transport systems. The first sod was cut in June 1876, and the track was inspected on 7 August of that year and declared safe and fit for purpose. That same day, the first passengers enjoyed the ride along the sea front.

In 1877, Lightfoot bought property at the north end of the promenade and built stables that are still there today. Walking from the main road into the cobbled courtyard is to walk out of the 21st century into the 19th, so little seems to have changed – though in fact the stables have been enlarged over time. Otherwise, life here goes on much as it did in the past. The horses stand calmly in their stalls while the routine jobs of mucking out, adding fresh straw, grooming and providing feed carry on. There is even a forge, which is also much as it was, except that the air blast to the fire is now provided electrically, rather than by manually operated bellows. Shoeing, however, is carried out just as it always has been.

There have been changes over the years outside the stables. A second track was added, the route was extended and between 1895 and 1896 a new depot was built for the tramcars. This all happened during the system's heyday, when the trams were carrying over a million and

↑ The stables at Douglas.
← Meal time at the stables.
→ Harnessing up for a working shift.

PREVIOUS PAGES Preparing to shoe one of the horses that works the Isle of Man horse tram at Douglas.

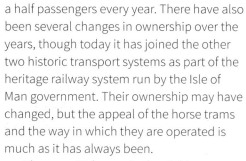

a half passengers every year. There have also been several changes in ownership over the years, though today it has joined the other two historic transport systems as part of the heritage railway system run by the Isle of Man government. Their ownership may have changed, but the appeal of the horse trams and the way in which they are operated is much as it has always been.

There are 21 horses in the stable, a mixture of Clydesdales and Shires, mostly purchased from a stud farm near Ramsey.

They are ideal for the job, powerful animals but with a very calm temperament. Visitors to the island can call in at the stables and see the animals, traditionally known as trammers. On a working day, depending on how busy the traffic is likely to be, two or three are brought out to work. They are harnessed up and taken out to the trams on the promenade. Animal welfare is a prime concern. Each horse does two runs, up and down, and is then replaced. And at the end of their working lives, they go to what is in effect a retirement home for horses where they can enjoy a peaceful life in green fields.

The cars are all vintage. The oldest was built in 1883 and was bought second-hand, while the oldest car bought new is No. 11,

of 1886. Altogether, 25 of the cars bought for the line still survive, all of which have already passed their hundredth birthdays. What is remarkable is that this, the largest historic collection of horse trams in the world, is made up not of museum pieces, but of cars still in active use. There are two basic types: those open for summer use, and those that are closed for winter. There are no turntables on the line; instead, the cars can be driven from either end. At the completion of each run, the horse is unhitched and walked round to the opposite end of the car for the return journey. The seats are specially designed with pivoted backs that can be pushed over so that passengers can always sit facing the way they are going.

Once the passengers are all on board, the driver takes his place at the front and the conductor stands at the back; then the journey can begin. The horses soon get into their stride at a steady trot, apparently quite oblivious to the noise and bustle of the traffic all around them. The passengers can admire the sea view to one side or, on the other, the handsome buildings lining the promenade. The grandest building is the Gaiety Theatre, built in 1900 by the most famous theatre designer of the age, Frank Matcham. But for most passengers it is not really the scenery or the architecture that enchants as much as the sheer pleasure of travelling in a horse-drawn vehicle just as their ancestors might have done more than a century ago.

THE STEAM RAILWAY

The horse tramway may be the oldest form of transport on the island, but it was not the first to be built there. In the 19th century, communities were clamouring to be connected by the wonderful power of steam, but the Isle of Man was quite late to join the fray.

The Steam Railway Company was formed in 1870, and the first line, now abandoned, was completed to Peel and built to the same 3ft gauge as the horse tramway would be a few years later. The next section, to Port Erin, was opened in 1874. It is difficult to imagine now, when it is just an attractive seaside resort, but originally this little town was planned as an important deep-water harbour. But at least it still has the railway – and the railway still has its original locomotives and rolling stock. The majority of the surviving engines were built by Beyer Peacock and were supplied between 1874 and 1908. Railway enthusiasts might like to know that they are all 2-4-0Ts. The carriages are of a similar vintage, and enthusiasts and non-enthusiasts alike might also like – indeed, need – to know that unlike modern carriages, these do not have corridors – which, of course, also means no loos.

The company had to maintain all its own engines and rolling stock, so it built extensive workshops at Douglas alongside the engine shed. Many of the old machines are still there and still in use, though now powered by electricity rather than by the handsome steam engine, which is preserved even though its working days are done. Keeping these elderly machines in running order is a formidable task, and on our visit, several engines and carriages were receiving attention. The 1874 locomotive No. 4 and the 1905 No. 10 were both stripped right down and their boilers had been removed. The locomotive that was to take me as one of the passengers was No. 8 Fenella, built in 1894. She is typical of Victorian design, with a narrow, tall chimney, highly polished brass dome and prominent safety valve, and altogether a very attractive lady indeed.

The process of working the engine begins with lighting the fire

and slowly raising the steam up to working pressure. Before the start of the journey the fireman has the job of filling the bunker at the back of the cab with coal. That may sound simple, but he has to work from a heap of coal beside the track, dig out a shovelful and throw it into the narrow bunker. Our fireman had obviously had a great deal of practice. With that job complete, and with water on board and steam raised, it is time to join the line of carriages in Douglas station. Stepping into the compartment, everything is much as it has always been, with wood panelling and sash windows, let up and down by a leather strap. Fortunately, the seats have been reupholstered and offer a comfortable ride. The end coach has a compartment for the guard, with lookout windows at the side. There has been modernisation along the track. The old signal box with its rows of levers is still there but is no longer in use, having been replaced by the more modern electric system that also works barriers at level crossings. But apart from that, very little has changed since the last century and even further back.

↑ Out in the country between Castletown and Port Erin.

↓ Shovelling coal into the firebox.

PREVIOUS PAGES Isle of Man steam railway locomotives, No.8 *Fenella* of 1894 and No. 13 *Kissack* of 1908, getting up steam at the start of the working day.

A glance at an Ordnance Survey map of the island shows straight away that building a line here was never going to be simple. Everywhere there is a squirming mass of contour lines, indicating a landscape of

hills and hummocks through which the engineers would have to find a way. They took two approaches: where the hillocks were not too high, they simply cut through them; where they presented too great an obstacle, they set off on a wander round them. The length of the line is 15½ miles, but for a well-directed crow it's a mere 11 miles. That gives a good idea of what to expect.

On leaving the station there is a contrast in views: to one side is an attractive little river with wooded banks; to the other, dull industrial estates. But all that is soon left behind and the scenery becomes much more varied. At times you plunge into deep wooded cuttings, and as the line is only single track, the branches practically scrape the windows. It is, however, very pleasant to see such a large expanse of broadleaved woodland. Cuttings give way to a gently undulating landscape of fields and rough pasture, grazed by sheep and cattle. The nature of the track can be heard in the beat of the locomotive, puffing hard as it climbs and giving out a gentle whisper as it coasts downhill. Perhaps it is this response to the terrain, which is so similar to our own, that makes locomotives seem to have human characteristics. And that may also be why people seem to enjoy the sight of a steam train so much – almost everyone seems compelled to wave a greeting as it goes by. There are three halts between Douglas and Castletown, the next important station on the line. At one of these, Port Soderick, the line swings briefly down to the coast, offering sea views. There is a passing loop at Castletown, so there is a chance to see another locomotive hauling its train en route

from Port Erin. From the photographer's point of view, as Rob Scott discovered, this is not necessarily a great photo opportunity. As with the horse tram, the engines are not turned at the end, so the train arrives hauled by a locomotive travelling in reverse, presenting a view of little more than a slab of metal at the back of the cab.

The next leg of the journey is through a very pleasant rural landscape with an occasional foray into more shady cuttings, as the line takes a great curving route round

....

↓ Trains passing at Castletown station.

to the end of the line at Port Erin. The railway station is an attractive little building, built, unusually for this area, in bright red brick, with an ornate canopy at the front. Next to it is the railway museum for all those who want to know more about this very delightful line. There may be other preserved railways that can boast grander, more powerful locomotives, and perhaps even more dramatic scenery, but there are very few that offer this authentic glimpse into the past: there is nothing moving on this line that would not have been familiar to a Victorian traveller.

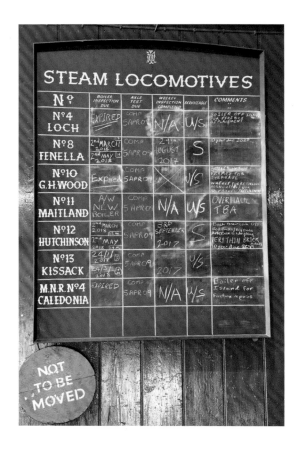

↑ The roster board
shows which of the
company's locomotives
is available for duty.

→ Filling the
bunker with coal
for the first journey
of the morning.

THE ELECTRIC TRAM

When Michael Faraday demonstrated how to obtain an electric current and then showed how it could be used to produce mechanical movement, he had actually provided the basis for both the generator and the electric motor.

But no one besides Faraday seemed to be aware of the implications at the time. When Prime Minister Gladstone asked him what use this electricity was, he gave the sort of answer that pleases politicians: 'Why, Sir, there is every possibility that you may soon be able to tax it!' It was not until the late 19th century that the full implications and possibilities of electrical power became evident. In 1884, the first electric tram, its power provided by a trolley running on overhead lines, went into service in Germany. By 1891 Leeds had the first British version. Unlike the steam railway, which came quite late to the island, the Isle of Man was off the mark quickly when it came to trams. Plans had been agreed for a new housing development north of Douglas, with the proviso that the developers had to supply a transport system. They decided that, given the success of the horse tram, a modern electric tram might be appropriate. This was in 1892, just one year after Leeds had shown the way. By the summer of 1893 the first short section had been completed as far as Groudle, and the Manx Electric Railway was in business.

The first season was quite short, just 17 days, but in that time 20,000 passengers were carried. This was encouragement enough to plan a major extension, and by 1899 the route had been opened all the way to Ramsey. And this is the line that still operates today. The depot at Derby Castle, at the end of the promenade, near the horse tram stables, still has its original tram shed, but new buildings and workshops have been added over the years. There was originally a powerhouse here to supply the line, but that has now just become part of the workshop complex.

The vehicles used today are a mixture of powered cars fitted with modern air brakes and unpowered trailers with hand brakes. There are two main types: open trams for summer use and closed ones for winter and bad weather. As with the steam railway, the old trams and trailers require a great deal of maintenance. But recently the permanent staff have had some help from volunteers who took on the task of assisting with restoring one of the trailers, which has now been stripped down to its wooden skeleton. It is a tribute to the carpenters who worked on building this coach over a century ago that the frame is still in magnificent condition. What is even more remarkable is that trams that were supplied when the line started are still in use, right back to No. 1 of 1893. There are a number of other differences between them. Some have longitudinal seating, where the passengers face each other – not exactly ideal for enjoying the scenery. Others have cross seating; like the horse trams, these seats have reversible backs that can be swung across so that everyone always faces the front. There is one rather special car, the directors' saloon, that has been known as the Royal Coach ever since it was used to carry Edward VII and Queen Alexandra on a trip. The tram itself is conventional enough, but the seating is far more luxurious than that enjoyed by paying passengers.

When the Manx government took over the running of the trams, the decision was made to change the 'old-fashioned' Victorian livery to something more modern – and a uniform

PREVIOUS PAGES The Manx Electric Railway provides passengers with fine seaside views.

← The interior of one of the vintage carriages, built over a century ago.

→ Restoring a vintage carriage.

dull green was chosen. No one liked it and the old colours were soon brought back – though one car has been kept with its green coat as a reminder of what happened in the 1950s. There is also one goods wagon in the collection. In the early days, the trams had an extra duty – they collected the mail from boxes all along the line. This is a remarkable collection of vintage vehicles, and Tram No. 1 can claim to be the oldest electric tram in the world still working on the line for which it was built.

At the start of the 17-mile trip, tram and trailer are brought from the shed and the trolley is swung across by a rope to be

attached to the overhead power lines. Then there is a short trip down to the booking office to collect the passengers before setting off on the journey to Ramsey. Trams have fewer problems with hills than steam locomotives do, so there are fewer engineering challenges involved in laying out the line. Right from the start there's a coast-hugging climb up to Onchan Head and the line stays close to the road, but with views

out to sea as far as the original destination of Groudle, this really sets the theme for most of the journey: for anyone who enjoys extensive sea views, this line offers plenty for a good part of the way. And even when the sea is left behind, there are still fine views to enjoy of fields and more distant hills.

At Groudle the line is forced to swerve inland to avoid the deep cleft of Groudle Glen. The line then remains inland, taking a more or less direct route to Baldrine. After that it's back to sea views again on the next leg to Laxey. Here, once again, the line is forced to take a right-angled turn to run

along one side of the deep valley. But this provides an opportunity to look down on the town's most famous industrial monument, the Laxey Wheel. The overshot waterwheel is 72ft 6in in diameter, the world's biggest, and was built in 1854 to drive pumps to clear water from the Great Laxey Mine. The deep mine produced mainly lead, with silver and zinc. It has long since closed down, but the wheel has been preserved and visitors can climb to the top to admire the view, or simply to marvel at the engineering required for anything this massive.

Laxey is also the starting point for the Snaefell Mountain Railway, the second electric line built on the island. Instead of the standard 3ft gauge, this one is 3ft 6in because it has to incorporate a third rail down the centre of the track. This line uses a system devised by the engineer John Barraclough Fell for the much more demanding task of getting locomotives over the Mont-Cenis pass in the Alps. The engines were fitted with an extra pair of wheels, mounted horizontally and gripping the centre rail to provide extra traction for the climb. It worked in the Alps, and it works too with the electric trams here as they make their way to the summit station at 621 metres, the highest point on the island.

From Laxey, the route continues northwards for its most spectacular section, running high above the cliffs, before turning back inland again, only rejoining the coast on the approach to Ramsey. For anyone who thinks that trams were only built for city streets, this is a revelation, providing a ride through some of the most attractive countryside the island has to offer. It was a fitting end to a visit to three historic transport systems, which between them covered the whole gamut of changes that transformed travel in 19th-century Britain.

FAIRS AND ENTERTAINMENTS

APPLEBY
HORSE FAIR

Early in June every year the peaceful town of Appleby-in-Westmorland is transformed by the arrival of thousands of Gypsies and Travellers, their numbers swelled by the crowds of spectators who come to enjoy the spectacle of the horse fair.

Many of the families arrive in traditional horse-drawn hooped wagons, others in more conventional caravans. But everyone, it seems, brings horses. The fair is at once a major opportunity to trade and an important social event, the biggest gathering of Gypsies and Travellers in Europe. And the trading is a serious matter, with huge amounts of money changing hands. Bargaining is a very public event, the seller and the potential buyer haggling noisily, spurred by a ring of spectators who encourage one or the other with language that can best be described as colourful. Each offer is accompanied by a slap of hands until a final price is agreed. That is then a deal done, perhaps for thousands of pounds, and it is followed by a ritual wishing of good luck all round – and that's important too, a courtesy never to be overlooked.

There have been fairs here for centuries, but originally they were very different affairs, with livestock being traded between the local farmers. The whole project withered for a time, but the tradition was revived late in the 19th century as 'the new fair', still largely for livestock. It was only in the early 20th century that the Travellers began to arrive from all over Britain with their horses, and today it has become very much their event. But it is still the horses that are at the heart of everything. If you want to sell a horse, you want it to look at its best. The harness must be perfect and gleamingly bright. The animals themselves are washed in the river and often brushed down with talcum powder that removes any greasiness from the hide. Manes are brushed, tails plaited and the horses are ready to go on display. Many of them are bred for trotting races, and the spindly trotting carts race

← Washing horses in the River Eden at Appleby *(far left)*; two men bargaining *(left)*; a farrier at work at Appleby *(bottom left)*; horse and trap racing up near Hangingshaw Hill. *(bottom left and right)*.

PREVIOUS PAGES A traditional caravan on its way to the Appleby Horse Fair.

OVERLEAF The boys show off to the girls and the girls show off to the boys.

each other down the streets of the town at high speed between pavements and verges crowded with onlookers.

This is a major social event for the Travelling communities, and traditionally one where weddings were arranged. Such arranged marriages might not be quite the thing these days, but for the young men and women of these communities, it is still certainly an opportunity to show off to the opposite sex – and what better way to dc that than by getting on a horse and plunging into the river? The lads show off their prowess, standing up on the horses' backs as they make their way through the water; and the

young women will often be just as keen to ride bareback into the river. It may all be more than a touch ostentatious, but what is obvious to even the least knowledgeable spectator is that the members of this community know and understand horses and can manage them with consummate skill.

Fairs were once a vital element in the life of the countryside. There were hiring fairs, where workers would be signed up for the whole of the following year, as well as the usual livestock fairs. And where so many people were gathered together and enjoying what was often a holiday atmosphere, there was always a demand for entertainment.

There might have been groups of strolling actors performing short plays on very basic stages. There might have been jugglers and acrobats entertaining the crowd and passing round with a hat to collect money. And there would have been entertainments for the children, perhaps nothing more sophisticated than a roundabout worked by hand. But from these modest beginnings we have travelling theatres, funfairs and circuses. And the one thing they all have in common is music in some form or other.

↑ Everyone wants to show off their horses as spectacularly as possible.

→ Bargains are made all over town – offers are made and rejected, then hands are slapped to clinch a deal and the celebrations start.

THE FAIRGROUND ORGAN

It would have been too expensive to get a whole band of experienced and skilled musicians together to produce the sound of a full orchestra just to amuse a fairground crowd. But a solution was found in the 19th century – a mechanical organ was specifically designed for use at fairs to accompany rides and attract customers to the shows.

At the most fundamental level, the fairground organ works on the same principle as the familiar church organ: musical notes are produced by blowing air through pipes. But that is about all they have in common. Where the older church organ is played either to hushed congregations in churches or to attentive audiences in concert halls, the fairground organ has to make its presence felt amid the raucous bustle of noisy crowds and showpeople competing for attention. There is not much room for subtlety here: this is an instrument that is going to be hauled all over the country and that must make a sound with mass appeal. The musical model on which it is based is not the symphony orchestra but the military band. There are violin pipes to help supply the main melody, but the emphasis is very much on instruments such as saxophones, clarinets, trumpets and trombones, with drum accompaniment. And, of course, as well as having to attract attention by the sound they make, fairground organs must also shout out visually – so they generally have cases decorated with gilded swags, and animated figures conduct the band or strike bells in front of the organ case.

These organs were immensely popular in the late 19th century and well into the 20th, and it might have been expected that they would long since have been overtaken by more sophisticated technology. But somehow their attraction has never died, in part due to the appeal of their unique and instantly recognisable sound, and also partly because their over-the-top decoration brings a welcome touch

of extravagance and colour to the world. There is still a demand for new fairground organs of various types and sizes – and in Britain that demand is met, as it has been for three generations, by the Dean family.

The Deans have a long history of craftsmanship, with generations of master craftsmen going as far back as John Dean, a cabinet maker working in Bridport in 1818. The family moved to the Bristol area in 1899, and Edwin Dean took on the present workshops in Whitchurch in 1939. It was here that Edwin's son Michael began manufacturing fairground organs, later to be joined by his son Richard. When Michael retired, Richard took over the business, and now he has been joined by his son Tom.

Given that fairground organs are among the most elaborate musical instruments ever made, with their ornate frontages and pirouetting figurines, it might be expected that something similar might be reflected in the workshops where they are built. But not a bit of it. Whitchurch was once no doubt a town with a character of its own, but it has long been swallowed up into suburban Bristol, and the workshops just off the main road look like any small-scale industrial buildings of a certain age. Stepping inside, there is the familiar working environment of organised clutter. Various machine tools, lathes, drills and milling machines stand against the walls, and the walls themselves seem covered with hand tools of all sorts. Nothing has ever been thrown away here: some of those tools are Richard Dean's; others belonged to his father and some to his grandfather. At first glance there is not much to distinguish this from other small engineering or carpentry workshops. But where there is a space left among the tools, there are photos of organs, some faded, some new. Organ pipes are scattered around

→ Richard Dean at work constructing a brand new fairground organ.

PREVIOUS PAGES
The Dean bioscope at the Dorset Steam Fair.

← Tom Dean painting one of the animated figures that go on the front of an organ.

→ The ornate front of the bioscope organ.

the benches, and in the centre of the main rooms are objects shrouded in dust covers; a peep beneath one reveals a barrel organ waiting for renovation, and under another is a small organ. It is only when you talk to Richard and Tom that you realise what a truly magical place this is. Literally everything that goes into a new organ is built by them: the individual pipes, the mechanism, the decoration, the animated figures – the whole lot. Building an organ requires an astonishing array of skills – woodworking, metalworking, painting, carving – and musical ability. It also requires enthusiasm and willingness to engage in hard work – qualities Richard and Tom have in plenty.

The organ pipes of either wood or metal are made on the premises. Wood is used for the pipes emulating instruments such as violins and flutes, while the saxophone and clarinet pipes are fitted with little reeds to create the appropriate sound. The pipes for brass instruments are generally made of metal. Whatever material is used, they all have to be accurately tuned, and in some of the bigger organs they make here there can be as many as 550 individual pipes. The basic mechanism for producing the sound

consists of a wind chest, into which air is blown by bellows. This air has to be passed via pipes and valves to the appropriate organ pipes, and these have to be positioned into accurately drilled holes in the wind chest.

The outer casing shows that the cabinet-making skills of the Dean forebears have been passed down to the present generation. Then the decoration has to be added. This can be carved out of wood or made from moulds. But the real distinguishing feature between these and other organs takes us back to the fairground story. The whole purpose of the organ was to pull in the customers to the show or the ride, but the showmen were not going to be paying an organist to sit there all day and night, pounding on the keys. These organs had to be automatic. And this was only made possible by the advent of the electric motor – and here again, it was often the dynamo on a showman's engine that supplied the power.

A system has been developed that uses punched cards to control the instrument. Greatly simplified, the process is as follows: once the bellows start working, the wind chest becomes filled with air under pressure. The holes in the chest are fitted with light 'puff' valves that are easily pushed up by the air, but they are also attached to thin metal spindles. When a card passes over the chest, it pushes the spindles down, closing off the air supply, but where holes are left, the air is free to move into the appropriate pipes. Preparing these cards is a vital part of the organ builder's job. This has now largely been taken over by Tom.

The starting point for the music is the conventional score. The one that Tom was working on was in a key that was inappropriate for the organ, so he transposed it into a more appropriate one, in this case C major, the simplest of them all, with no flats or sharps. Now he needed to orchestrate it: the melody would be apportioned to one set of instruments, perhaps violins and saxophones, the bass line to the low tones of the double bass and trombone, and a counter melody added, perhaps in the form of little runs above the main line on the high-pitched piccolo. Once this had been done, a diagram had to be prepared to show where each hole must go and how long it has to be. When the actual cards are produced, they will pass through the organ at the steady rate of 3.6 metres a minute, which means that if a long note has to be held for a whole second, it will need a slit exactly 60cm long. Once the pattern is complete it can be used to cut the holes in the card. This is done by hand, and the finished cards are fastened together; as the total length for just a simple three-minute piece adds up to 10.8 metres, they can be

↓ A Dean organ attracts young admirers at Giffords Circus.

concertinaed to form a convenient book. So the cards are pulled across one at a time, and then collapse back again into a compact pile after they have been played.

The work of making the initial pattern is now done with the help of a computer program, which has the added advantage that it can play the music as the pattern is formed. In the old days, however, it was all down to the individual's knowledge and experience: he had to hear the sounds in his head and hope they came out as he had imagined them. It still requires skill and musicianship – when Tom's not doing this, he plays the bass. But there is no computer program for cutting out the holes – that is still done by hand, a job that must require infinite patience. It is interesting comparing the finished patterns with more familiar-looking musical scores; for example, on some you can see a pattern of a long hole and two short holes in the bass end, a giveaway that this is the oom-pah-pah 6/8 beat of the waltz. Almost any kind of music can be used: one client was a Status Quo fan who wanted their songs adapted for the organ, which must at least have been relatively straightforward, and Tom even wrote a special number for his grandad, who used to be a drummer in a dance band – a foot-tapping boogie-woogie of the sort he'd have been playing in the 1940s.

The complexity of a great fairground organ is staggering. There is so much detail to produce just the right effect. A popular figurine that appears on these instruments is the band master, and in a sophisticated organ the movement of his arm with the baton is geared to the rhythm of the bass, so that he always beats in time – and when the music changes direction, the tune passing to different instruments, he turns his head, as if looking to see where the sound is coming from.

And, yes, they make these figures here as well.

Organs come in a variety of different sizes. One of the most popular uses for them at the fair was on the steam gallopers, but as the organs were generally placed in the centre of the ride, where space was limited, they had to be quite small and therefore comparatively simple. But they can be really huge affairs, and Richard started building a monster for his own satisfaction some 15 years ago – he and Tom hope to have it finished soon. And there was always one fairground show that had

↑ A book of punched cards that are fed into the organ – the position of a hole allows air to go through a specific pipe and the size determines the length of the note.

room in plenty for a really big organ – namely, the bioscope. Cinematography was invented in the late 19th century, and long before cinemas were being built to show them, films were brought to the general public in travelling shows via the bioscopes. These became popular fairground attractions,

combining short films with live entertainment – and the great organ was not just a front-of-house draw, but an essential part of the whole show. One of the biggest attractions at Britain's biggest steam fairs, held each year in Dorset, is the Dean bioscope – comprising a magnificent organ, short silent films and dancers. It is difficult to imagine a better use for a wonderful musical instrument that is also a mechanical marvel and a huge credit to the ongoing craftsmanship of the Dean family of organ builders.

THE CIRCUS

Walking across the big village green at Frampton-on-Severn, the sound of a Dean fairground organ drifts across, while up ahead a ring of brightly painted showman's wagons circles the big top, holding out the promise of a truly traditional circus treat. And that is exactly what you will get with a visit to Giffords Circus.

The circus itself has only been going since 2000, but from the start its originators, Nell and Toti Gifford, wanted to create the feel and atmosphere of a show from the early part of the 20th century. It all began when Nell Stroud, as she was then, took a year off before going to university.

She told the story in *Josser*, her wonderful account of working in a circus, published in 1999 – for the uninitiated, a josser is a circus worker who doesn't come from a traditional circus family. She got a job in an American circus, and although it was immensely hard work, she fell in love with the whole idea. Nevertheless, she went up to Oxford, took her degree, and then promptly started looking for another circus job. She worked for a number of circuses in Britain and Europe, and several themes emerge from the book. The most obvious is the sheer dedication of everyone who works in the shows, in whatever capacity. Then there was the realisation that while the circus was valued as a genuine art form in Continental Europe, it was not treated with the same respect in Britain. The third point that comes across strongly is that the circus is an international affair in which performers from many different countries can work together. Nell got married to Toti Gifford, and they immediately decided that they wanted to start a circus of their own. They were very sure of what they wanted to achieve.

The early years were a struggle. They were working on a minuscule budget, but they received a positive impetus when Nell was asked to the Hay-on-Wye literary festival to promote her book. She suggested that rather than turn up and just talk, she should bring the circus. The organisers were delighted, and Nell and Toti now had a deadline – the show had to be ready for May 2000. The start was difficult, but

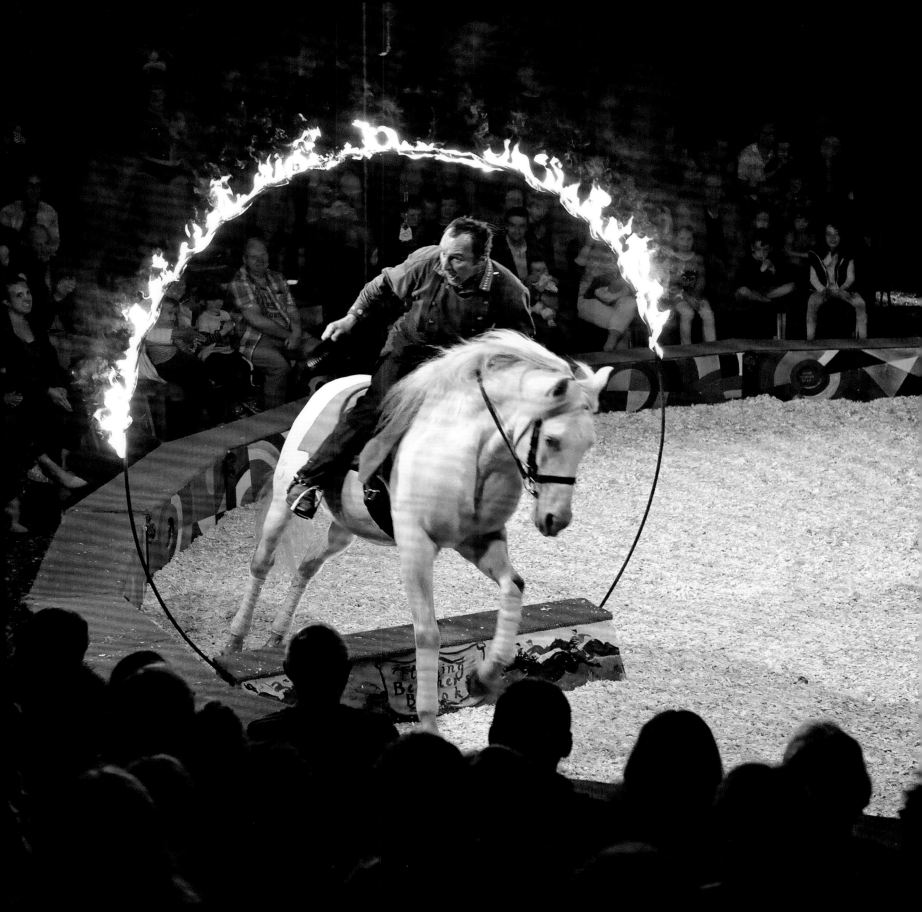

←↖ Circus skills are learned young – mastering the art of juggling *(top left)*; the clown Tweedy practising his skills *(centre left)*; keeping fit is essential for performers – they encourage and help each other with weight training *(bottom left)*.

↑ Two of the Ethio Wingets having fun at practice.

→ Most of the cast travel in traditional circus caravans.

PREVIOUS PAGES Giffords Circus is completely traditional – a ring inside a tent.

over the years the reputation of Giffords Circus spread: audiences grew and more venues were added. Slowly the circus itself evolved, and instead of simply being a number of different acts strung together, each year had a specific theme, which translated into the backdrop to the show, the music and the costumes, and gave everything a colourful unity. In 2016, for example, the theme was the Western saloon, while 2017 was a complete contrast. The artistic vision was the Spanish Baroque, in particular the work of the great painter Velásquez. Images from his famous painting *Las Meninas* – the

maids of honour – was the inspiration for all the design aspects, including the backdrop, which contained images from the painting, and the costumes, seen at their exotic best in the opening parade. One element that was present from the start was live music, and for the Spanish show the band was required to play in a variety of genres, including baroque, and they were joined by a singer; there must be few circuses in the world where horses perform in the ring to the accompaniment of Vivaldi's *Gloria*.

....

↓ The Ethio Wingets relaxing.

Running a circus requires a great deal of organisation. When it first started, the office was a garden shed, but today they have their own headquarters in a building on a farm just outside Stroud in Gloucestershire, and a team to help. Work starts on the next show during the summer, and once the theme has been discussed and a decision made, designer Louise Birkin begins to work with Nell on designs for scenery and graphics, but not costumes. She originally studied film production and was working in art departments on short films and fashion shoots when she saw the circus advert,

applied and got the job. That was six years ago. During the winter, various activities are carried out, such as repair to the traditional wagons that are such a featurre of the circus. Then a lot of decisions have to be taken. The music director, James Kay, will work with the show director to decide on the type of music needed and whether the musicians from the previous year should be asked back or whether a different type of sound is needed. The music is vital, and choosing the right sound is essential. Sometimes the result happens more or less by accident. One year Nell was in Paris when she heard a group of French music students busking in the street. She followed them and invited them to join the circus for the summer. Not surprisingly, they agreed. I saw that particular show, and it was interesting to see the way in which the musicians not only played wonderfully lively music but were involved in the ring as well. They looked as if they were having the time of their lives.

Every aspect of the show to come has to be considered, and meetings are held with everyone involved to work out lighting, sound, costumes and acts. Now that there is

↑ Aline Shipynova texting and stretching.

→ Tweedy in contemplative mood.

OVERLEAF The artistes Duo Lyrical Lyra combine athleticism with grace.

a wardrobe department at the headquarters, many of the costumes are made on site, but some are made outside and brought in for the finishing touches to be added. Then it is a question of which of the current acts should be invited back next year and how their performances can be adapted to the new theme. New acts might also need to be selected. Once everything is agreed, there is a hectic period in the spring when all the elements have to come together and be rehearsed ready for the opening. The opening is always on the farm and then the show goes out on the road – and in August

2017 it arrived at Frampton-on-Severn.

Every available seat was filled when we visited, and because the tent is comparatively small there is a real feeling of intimacy. This is something the performers all encourage, not least the clown, Tweedy, who has been with Giffords for many seasons. His inspiration was the great silent comedians such as Buster Keaton, and rather less obviously, animated cartoons. His first thought for a career was to go to art school to study animation, but then he realised he didn't want to create characters – he wanted to be those characters himself. And there was

only one place where he could achieve that – the circus. He had hoped to join the circus school but it closed down before he had the chance. So he sent out a questionnaire to all the clowns he could think of, asking for advice. He got a reply from the clown Zippo saying there was only one way to learn how to be a clown – join the circus and find out by being one. So he seized the chance to join Zippo's troupe in a minor role, doing jobs such as handing out leaflets in the street to advertise the show while dressed and made up as a clown. Then one day, Zippo himself got held up in traffic and couldn't make

↑ The grand finale.

→ Members of the Ethio Winget Troupe performing.

the show, giving Tweedy his chance in the ring. Zippo was back in time to catch the end of Tweedy's act, liked it, and his career had begun in earnest. At this stage he was a typical Auguste clown, with a big red nose and extravagant make-up. When he applied to and was accepted by Giffords, Nell said she wasn't happy with his character. He was delighted, because neither was he – and the traditional clown make-up was abandoned.

Tweedy's act has a touch of the surreal about it – he is first in the ring with an iron on the end of a leash as if it were a pet, high-fiving the kids in the audience and setting the mood. He has a whole variety of skills and, unlike some clowns, is genuinely funny, appealing as much to adults as to children. He reappears at various points in the show – often when he shouldn't be there, according to the ringmaster – and at one point he was chased off by a pecking chicken. Animal acts, apart from horses, are no longer part of the circus scene – but Giffords does have performing hens.

The acts that follow are all notable for the immense skill of the performers – the jugglers, the aerialists, the acrobats and the horse riders. What appeals is that they do not simply present their special skills but turn in complete performances, so that the audience gets throughly involved and tries to persuade the artists to go for ever greater feats – which, of course, they were going to do anyway. The comparatively small tent is actually an advantage – in one act involving a swing, the performers use the device to gain momentum so that they can fly off, pirouetting and somersaulting in the air, seemingly right over the heads of the crowd. This act typifies the diversity of the show – these aerial artists have come from Cuba. And for many of the urban children in the audience, being almost within touching distance of a cantering horse is a very special thrill.

Why is this circus so successful? Ultimately it's down to the quality of the individual acts – acts that are honed by endless practice. Walking round before the show, we found some of the men lifting weights and egging each other on to go for more lifts, heavier weights. Often what you are seeing is performers who combine great athletic ability with artistry – and it is this combination that makes the show so popular with all ages. There is no doubt, too, that having a unified theme where everything comes together – live music, design and performances – makes this circus very special. And there is also the irresistible allure of tradition, the atmosphere that is created before you even step inside the big top. It all forms a most satisfying whole, a complete experience. Nell Gifford was concerned when she first started out in circus that its artistry was not appreciated in Britain – it most certainly is now.

PUNCH AND JUDY

The seaside Punch and Judy show on the beach seems a quintessentially British summer scene, yet it has its origins on the other side of Europe, in Italy.

It began with the Commedia dell'arte in the 16th century. This consisted of dramas, unusual for the time in that both male and female actors took part, and though the scripts might change over the years, most of the characters remained standardised. The best known of these are Pierrot and Columbina, who provided the romantic interest, while most of the comedy came from Pulcinella. Like many of the Commedia characters, he was always portrayed in a mask, and his had a beak-like nose – hence the name, which comes from 'pulcino', or chick. He was also usually portrayed with a fat belly, a humped back and a squeaky voice, and he carried a cudgel. He was the rogue who always seemed somehow or other to come out on top.

The plays were immensely popular and many of the characters were adopted for puppet shows, Pulcinella among them. In 1662 the puppeteers for one of these shows, Pietro Grimade, known as Signor Bologna, brought the show to England and put on a performance at Covent Garden in London that was visited on 9 May by Samuel Pepys, who wrote in his diary: 'there to see an Italian puppet play that is within the rayles there which is very pretty, the best that ever I saw.' Pulcinella was a central character, but his name had been changed for an English audience – he was now Punchinella. It is generally agreed that this was the origin of our Mr Punch. But this was certainly not the Punch we know – for the early versions were marionettes on strings, not glove puppets. And originally Judy was Joan – and there was another female character, Pretty Polly, with whom Punch was having an affair. These were shows mainly intended for an adult audience.

Gradually the show evolved to the one we know today. Pulcinella's beak became a hooked nose almost meeting an upturned chin, and the cudgel became a stick. To make it more effective when used in the play, a special version was used, consisting of two pieces of wood hinged together at one end so that they made a loud slapping noise – hence its name, the slapstick, which would later become used for any form of knockabout comedy. Pulcinella's squeaky voice became

harsher for Mr Punch and was produced using a swazzle – a device consisting of a reed held between two metal plates that the puppeteer holds in the mouth. There was one other change – Mr Punch was no longer dressed in the floppy white costume of an Italian comic character; instead, he wore the brightly coloured clothes of an English jester. Over the years most of the other connections

with the Italian original faded away too. The wistful Pierrot and flirty Columbina disappeared, and new comic characters were added, including the very unlikely resident of a British seaside resort, a crocodile. So gradually all the different elements came together. What had once been a show that appealed as much to adults as to children became entirely aimed at the latter. The

seaside shows took place in brightly coloured booths and always used glove puppets. The story elements became more or less standardised and remain much the same today as they were a century ago. Punch is an anarchic figure, hopelessly untrustworthy and more than happy to resort to violence. He has always been attacked by the more puritanical elements in society, but children

love seeing someone behaving really badly and getting away with it. When left to look after the baby, he promptly loses it, and when Judy berates him, he whacks her with the slapstick. Told to mind the sausages, he fails to notice a crocodile creeping up to snatch them – though of course the kids all shout to warn him. And when the authorities appear to punish him for his misdeeds, they get whacked as well. It is always a scene of glorious mayhem.

Once, not that long ago, you could expect to find a Punch and Judy show on the beach of any big seaside resort. Today they are sadly rare, but one man at least is carrying on the tradition. Mark Poulton was brought up in Gloucestershire and the family used to go to their nearest seaside resort, Weston-super-Mare, for their holidays. It was there, as a young boy in the 1970s, that he saw his first show. But it was when they ventured a little further afield to Weymouth that he saw Professor Guy Higgins' Punch and Judy show and watched it over and over again. The title of professor indicates that Higgins was a member of the Punch and Judy College, an institution that, in its own words, is 'as academic as a school of whales and as organised as a string of sausages'. But membership of the college was a guarantee that the professor had thoroughly learned the art and craft of Punch and Judy. It was then, as a small boy, that Mark decided that when he grew up he would be a Punch and Judy man too.

Not having a glove puppet to work with, he ripped open his teddy bear, pulled out the stuffing and used the disembowelled soft toy instead, doing his own version of the show he had seen over and over again on the beach. He made his own makeshift booth to do shows for the neighbours in the garden and gradually improved on the original

← Professor Mark Poulton with his two stars.

↑ Relaxing after a show.

PREVIOUS PAGES Mark Poulton's traditional Punch and Judy show on the beach at Weymouth.

performances with the mutilated teddy. His enthusiasm paid off in 1987 when, at the age of just 15, he was able to do shows with Bill Dane at Aberystwyth. That same year he won a competition and was awarded the title of 'Most Promising Young Professor', which was a huge boost to his confidence. As a result, he was invited by Mrs Codman to use her booth at Llandudno for the summer season.

In 1989 Mark passed his driving test, left school and decided to set up in business on his own. Seventeen-year-olds don't generally find it an easy matter to raise funds, so there was no money with which to buy equipment. If he wanted his own show, he would have to provide everything himself. That meant learning how to carve his own puppets and sew and make their costumes. He had to

build his own booth, which consists of the gaily striped lower section behind which he works and the area where the puppets perform – the proscenium arch, which, like its large theatrical namesake, has curtains to open and close a show. That year he had a season at Paignton in Devon and his career had begun. In 2005 he moved to Weymouth, to the beach where he had first been enchanted by Punch and Judy, and that is where he performs each summer right up to the present day. The shows are very traditional, with all the familiar characters, and there are parts where everyone can join in – a popular favourite is the boxing match, where the children are encouraged to take sides. He always has to assess his audience and be ready to adapt the show to make sure everyone has a good time.

The summer season on the beach is still at the heart of Mark's work, but it is not sufficient to provide an income for a whole year. Like other Punch and Judy professors, he also performs at special events and private parties, but he makes puppets for other performers too. A typical Punch comes in three sections. The main part of the head is made of lime from the slopes of Minchinhampton Common in Gloucestershire, while the separate nose and chin are carved from oak or ash. They are then painted and their costumes made – all of which he does himself. He also builds proscenium arches for other performers and holds workshops and educational classes. And as a sideline, he paints banners and displays. It is not an easy life and certainly not an occupation for anyone to take up who is looking to make a fortune, but he has the great satisfaction of being one of those rare individuals who has achieved his childhood dream. And, just as importantly, he is keeping a wonderful tradition alive.

THE THEATRE

Travelling shows of all kinds were an essential part of life in Britain for many centuries, but purpose-built theatres date back to Shakespeare's day. However, they reached a golden age of lavish splendour in the 19th century.

One of the finest examples in Britain is the Tyne Theatre and Opera House in Newcastle. Designed by a local architectural firm, it first opened its doors in 1867. The façade is elaborate, but scarcely more so than those of many other theatres; it is when one gets inside that the true magnificence is revealed. Three tiers of circles and galleries sweep round the auditorium. The boxes by the stage are flanked by caryatids and the huge domed roof is a masterpiece of elaborate plasterwork. Everything speaks of opulence, from the swagged curtains that top the proscenium arch to the polished brass of the circle railings. Some famous names offering a variety of entertainments can be found on programmes from the theatre's early days, from Oscar Wilde lecturing on fashion to a performance by the most famous female actor of the day, Sarah Bernhardt.

The theatre holds an audience of over a thousand, so attractions have to be very special to fill all those seats, and those who came here in the 19th century would have expected to find spectacles to match the surroundings. And they did! It is difficult for us to imagine the effect of some of these shows on audiences at the time. We are used to seeing anything from spaceships to massed armies on huge screens, or these days even on our smartphones. At a time when such devices were not even dreamed of, it was the theatre that had to supply the spectacular sights. Among the most amazing productions was *The Armada* of 1889, featuring a fleet of Spanish galleons being sunk by the intrepid British seadogs – an effect that involved 32 tons of props and scenery. Even that was surpassed by *The Prodigal Son*, featuring the Grand National – in which real horses thundered across the stage, leaping real hurdles. The production of such shows required a complex system of stage machinery, and this is where the Tyne Theatre's true importance lies, for much of that machinery still exists there.

← The lift that allows people or objects to pop up on the stage through a trapdoor.

→ Victorian stage machinery at the Tyne Theatre.

PREVIOUS PAGES
The auditorium of the Tyne Theatre and Opera House, Newcastle.

A backstage fire in 1985 destroyed the scenery fly tower – the space above the stage into which scenery can be hoisted out of sight of the audience and from which it can be lowered as required. It collapsed and damaged the machinery underneath, but not irreparably, and it has now been restored to its former glory. There is a whole set of different trapdoors in the stage, used to make things or characters appear or disappear – the pantomime demon can pop up in a cloud of smoke, for example, or Don Giovanni could sink to his fiery doom. They all have different names, from the ominous-sounding 'grave trap' to the curious 'carpet cut'. To work them there is a complex system of counterweights, blocks and ropes – the most complete set of Victorian stage machinery in Britain – which makes walking backstage rather like being on board a large sailing ship with unusually dense rigging and an array of winches. There is also a thunder-roll, a sloping metal trough down which cannonballs were originally rolled to produce a remarkably realistic thunder effect. Tragically, during one performance the cannonball leaped out of the trough, hit a stagehand on the head and killed him outright. After that incident, metal hoops were placed over the trough to prevent a repetition.

The theatre has had a chequered history. When the first movies appeared they offered something even newer and more startling than the most elaborate stage show, and the theatre was converted into a cinema. But technology continued to move on, and the spread of television reduced cinema audiences, with the result that this huge building became redundant. So it reverted to being a commercial theatre for a time and more famous names appeared – Placido Domingo sang here in *Tosca*, for example – but it was not a commercial success. However, it was far too valuable an asset to be left to go to ruin, so a charitable trust was set up to take it over and run it, as it still does. Today it is not just the performances that bring in the crowds – the unique theatre and its old and rather wondrous machinery themselves attract many groups of interested people too.

UP AND OVER

NEWCASTLE
SWING BRIDGE

Two problems have had to be dealt with by travellers throughout history: how to cross rivers, and how to get up steep slopes. The first has an obvious solution – a bridge.

The simplest type we still have in Britain is the clapper bridge, which simply consists of flat slabs of stone laid over roughly constructed stone piers. Over time, bridges became ever more complex, spanning far greater widths. But travel is not limited to those on land: for many, travelling by water is often just as important, and there are times when the different interests of the two parties clash. That is exactly what happened on the River Tyne in Newcastle in the middle of the 19th century.

William Armstrong was to become one of the leading inventors and manufacturers of the 19th century. His first important invention was the hydraulic crane, and in 1845 he persuaded the Newcastle city fathers that using such a device would greatly improve the turnaround time for ships at the quay. They agreed that he could build one as an experiment, but there was one other problem to overcome – that of water supply. He and his colleagues formed the Whittle Dene Water Company, which brought water down from the hills and supplied it under pressure to the citizens of Newcastle and Gateshead – and, of course, it was also used to provide water under pressure for the crane. In 1847 he established a factory upriver from Newcastle at Elswick, where he developed new and vastly improved methods for manufacturing large guns. But to make the business flourish, it was absolutely essential that big ships should be able to reach the wharf at Elswick – and this was where he had a problem.

The historic crossing point on the Tyne at Newcastle was directly below the castle that gives the city its name, and the castle in turn stands on the site of a Roman fort. An elegant nine-arch stone bridge had been built on the site at the end of the 18th century. It seemed perfectly adequate at the time, and allowed the local keels that

collected coal from the collieries upstream to pass with ease. It blocked the way, however, for anything bigger. So Armstrong came up with a solution. He persuaded the city to allow him to build a swing bridge that would pivot on a central island, allowing ample space either side for river traffic. His plans were accepted, but construction involved a great deal of work: Armstrong would actually need not just to build one literally revolutionary bridge, he would also have to provide a temporary bridge to carry the traffic while the old Georgian bridge was being demolished and the new one constructed.

Work began on the project in 1868, and the first question to be answered was how to provide the power to move such a vast structure. The obvious 19th-century answer was a large, powerful steam engine. However, the bridge would only be swung perhaps half a dozen times a day and there might be days when it wasn't required to be moved at all, but you can't turn a steam engine on and off, so it would have had to be kept

↑ The control room at the top of the swing bridge.

↓ The control tower.

PREVIOUS PAGES
The Newcastle swing bridge opening, with the high-level road and rail bridge in the background.

available all the time and regularly stoked for whenever it was needed. This was not an economic proposition. Armstrong, of course, had a better answer – hydraulic power. The system works because liquids, such as water, cannot be compressed, so pressure applied to fluid is transmitted equally through it in every direction. So if a huge amount of water is stored, and it is released through a small tube, it can exert a vast amount of pressure. This is something most of us are familiar with when we press lightly on the brake pedal of a car, yet easily bring a heavy mass of metal (ie the car) under control. Hydraulic systems of the time mostly used what were known as accumulators – tall water towers into which the liquid was pumped and then released through valves. The fact that there was no space on top of the bridge for such a tower didn't matter – it would work in exactly the same way wherever it was. So for the Newcastle swing bridge, the accumulator is not a tower but a deep iron-walled well below the central island. And it is on the central island that it all happens.

The bridge itself is an elegant but massive structure, 281 feet in length and weighing 1,450 tons. The mechanism for moving the beast is no less impressive. The hydraulic engine itself is a three-throw version, with three rams attached to the crankshaft. This connects through gears to a rack and pinion system on the actual rotating platform that carries the bridge, which moves on massive rollers. There are actually two identical engines so that if one breaks down or needs maintenance the other can be brought into play. They are normally kept out of gear but are easily brought into alignment by winding a handle that meshes them together via a worm screw.

The bridge master works at the top of the ornate tower that does look rather like a fancy gazebo on the bridge, but is strictly functional. It is high enough for him to have a clear view of everything around the bridge, and with windows all the way round, he has a complete 360° field of vision. In fact this is probably the best view of Newcastle and its river that you can find. The mechanism itself looks quite simple, just levers and a handle on a pedestal. Before the bridge can be moved, the ends have to be listed slightly by hydraulic jacks and steadied by blocks. Then the blocks can be removed by means of another lever and the handle turned to open the valve from the hydraulic system, and slowly the bridge begins its stately progress. Once under way, it moves under its own momentum. The normal direction of

motion is anticlockwise, and it only needs to turn through 180° to open up the passage to either side of the island, but on our visit we got the full revolution, as we were there on one of the regular testing days.

Not many big ships travel up the Tyne these days, so the bridge is only manned when a ship movement is logged in, but over the years it has been kept busy – it has been estimated that it has swung around 300,000 times. It is a tribute to Armstrong's engineering that the same hydraulic engines that were first used in July 1876, when the steamship *Europa* made her way up to Elswick to collect a heavy gun, are still in use today. For the millennium celebrations of 2000 a new bridge was built over the Tyne,

known locally as the blinking eye – and like Armstrong's original, it can be moved hydraulically to allow ships to pass. Where the original cost £240,000, the latest Tyne bridge was £22 million. Interestingly, though, if you compare what a pound could buy in 1876 with what it could buy in 2000, the difference between the two costs is quite small. Technology may have advanced a lot since Armstrong's day, but even without all the equipment available to modern engineers he was remarkably economical. And the two bridges have something else in common: not only are they great works of engineering, they are truly beautiful structures as well.

→ The 19th century hydraulic machinery that is used to move the bridge.

NEWPORT TRANSPORTER BRIDGE

In many ways the origins of this bridge are quite similar to those of the Newcastle swing bridge: it met the industrial need for a new river crossing that would not interfere with shipping.

Newport itself grew with the Industrial Revolution, during which coal mining and iron works rapidly developed in South Wales. These industrial sites were linked to Newport by the Monmouthshire Canal at the end of the 18th century, and as a direct result, docks were developed along the River Usk. The town prospered and the population grew to a point where new expansion had to take place to the east of the river – and that would require improved transport links. The local council considered the matter for some time, but by the 1890s traffic on the existing town bridge had become so congested that urgent action was needed. Matters were brought to a head when in 1896 John Lysaght of Wolverhampton announced his intention to build a massive steel works in South Wales. Newport was his first choice, but the company insisted on good road access, and unless that could be provided, it would move to an alternative site at Barry. Decisions needed to be made.

A number of options were considered. The idea of a tunnel was discarded as too expensive. A conventional bridge would have needed such extensive ramps to raise it to a height that would allow tall-masted ships underneath as to be wholly impractical. A swing bridge on the Newcastle pattern was ruled out because of the nature of the river: the Usk is tidal here and has the same rise and fall rates as the nearby Bristol Channel into which it empties, whose range is the second widest in the world. Building the necessary pier in the middle of the river would have been enormously difficult, and even if it could have been built, it would have been a hazard to shipping.

The river's own hazardous nature also made a ferry service too dangerous to consider for regular use. Fortunately, the Borough Engineer Robert Haynes was keeping up with the latest developments in technology and had heard of a new type of bridge developed by the French engineer Ferdinand Arnodin that seemed to be just the solution he was looking for.

Arnodin had patented the idea of a transporter bridge in 1887, and the very first to be built, at Bilbao, was the work of Arnodin himself and the Spanish engineer Alberto Palacio, who had been a pupil of Gustave Eiffel. The basic idea was to construct two tall towers, one on each bank of the river, and join them at their tops by a horizontal boom. A trolley, the traveller,

could run along the top of the boom, and a platform, the gondola, suspended underneath it could then carry passengers and vehicles at road level. The councillors of Newport were decidedly doubtful that such a strange-sounding contraption could possibly work, but Haynes took a party over to Rouen to see Arnodin's third, recently completed transporter bridge. It succeeded in convincing them, and in 1900 they applied to Parliament for permission to construct a similar structure at Newport. Permission was given and Arnodin and Haynes were appointed as joint engineers for the project, with Alfred Thorn of Westminster as contractor. Much of the design work was done in France, at Arnodin's headquarters at Châteauneuf-sur-Loire, which caused

a certain amount of difficulty for British engineers as the measurements were all metric, and they were working with imperial units. Nevertheless, work got under way – though it was never going to be an easy task.

The two towers are both shaped like an inverted 'V' and look almost flimsy when seen from a distance, rising to a height of 74 metres. They needed to be stabilised by cables – rather in the way that a tent pole is helped to stay upright by guy ropes fastened to pegs rammed into the ground. The difference is that with a bridge, everything has to be on a gargantuan scale. Each tower has four cables running from the top to ground level and each cable is made up of 127 steel wires, all of which have to be firmly anchored. So the first stage was to sink

← The electric motors that move the bridge carriage.

↗ The view from the gantry.

→ The bridge at night.

PREVIOUS PAGES
The Newport transporter bridge across the River Usk.

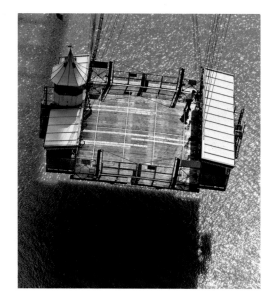

caissons, similar to those used at Newcastle, down into the ground until they reached bedrock, which turned out to be at a depth of 24 metres on one side and 26 metres on the other. Each of the four caissons was then filled with 2,236 tonnes of masonry to create a solid anchorage.

Once the towers were completed and secured the boom could be raised up, to be suspended from the top of the towers. Getting it in place was itself a great undertaking, since the towers are 180 metres apart and the main boom weighs in at 548 tonnes and finished up 54 metres above the high-water mark. The traveller is a 32-metre-long wheeled carriage that is hauled backwards and forwards by means of cables. These are powered by two 36-horsepower electric motors in the engine house on the east bank, which also houses the winding drum. A third motor was supplied for use as a standby in an emergency – no one wants to be left suspended over the River Usk. However, it has never been needed in the century and more that the bridge has been in use. The gondola that carries the traffic measures 10 metres by 12 metres.

Even today, the bridge seems an extraordinary edifice, massive and yet seemingly fragile. The main structure is strictly functional – no frills and ornaments here. The gondola is slightly more elaborate and decorated, and is fitted with iron gates at either end. Vehicles waiting to cross the bridge are kept behind ornate iron gates while the gondola trundles towards them. The control tower has a little pagoda roof, and there is a canopy to one side to provide shelter for foot passengers. The gondola moves at a sedate 3 metres a second, but as it was built in the age of the horse and carriage and before that of the horseless carriage, this speed would have seemed more than acceptable. Foot passengers don't have to be carried across on the gondola: they can instead choose to climb to the top and walk across – provided they don't mind panting up 280 steps. Rather surprisingly, some brave souls do that just to enjoy the view. They say

it's worth the effort. I believe them.

For almost a hundred years the transporter bridge had no rivals if you wanted to cross the river here, but the present century has seen the arrival of an alternative. There is no longer any shipping on the Usk, so a perfectly conventional road bridge has been built to carry the traffic. But happily the old bridge is still here and still working, simply because many people want the experience of gliding above the waters of the river, and its importance is recognised in its status as a Grade I listed structure. It even has its very own fan club – the Friends of Newport Transporter Bridge, volunteers who run the visitor centre on the west side. They are hoping to have new, much bigger premises in the not-too-distant future that will enable them to run proper educational classes. They deserve such facilities, and the bridge deserves to be celebrated as one of the engineering wonders of the world.

SALTBURN
CLIFF LIFT

Saltburn-by-the-Sea is a resort that would never have existed without the railways, and it was a railway contractor and engineer who helped bring it into being. The Stockton & Darlington Railway had promoted the Middlesbrough & Redcar Railway that opened in 1841, making Redcar a popular resort with workers from the industrial area surrounding the Tees.

A little way along the coast was the tiny hamlet of Saltburn-by-the-Sea, with nothing much there except for a wide, sandy beach. It was the entrepreneur John Pease who saw the possibility of turning a place that had previously been chiefly memorable as a haunt of smugglers into a fashionable resort: the working classes could go to Redcar, but only the wealthy would be catered for at Saltburn. The arrival of the railway in 1861 made this possible.

Pease turned to the railway contractor John Anderson, who had a long association with the Stockton & Darlington, to turn his plans into reality. Anderson not only agreed to work on various structures but made some astute investments of his own, purchasing land on the clifftop, where he built the Alexandria Hotel and the houses along Marine Drive, and the scene has changed very little since then. The terraces are based on those of Georgian spa towns such as Cheltenham, and sport ornate wrought-iron balconies – just the sort of thing to appeal to a wealthy clientele. Anderson was also responsible for constructing that essential feature of all Victorian seaside resorts – the pier. The planners, however, realised that they still had a problem – the visitors might be keen to walk down from their clifftop hotel to the beach, but they were less enthusiastic about struggling back up again. Anderson's answer was to build a lift. The first version was an extraordinary, flimsy-looking affair that seemed to have been constructed out of a giant Meccano set. A long gantry reached out from the clifftop to arrive at the vertical lift. It was cheap – just a halfpenny a

ride – but was soon declared to be unsafe. It was demolished and an alternative was built instead: the cliff railway.

The funicular railway is based on the water-balance system. Basically, two cars, joined together by cable, run on parallel tracks. Each car has a water tank underneath. The one at the top is filled with water, the one at the bottom emptied. The car with the full tank descends under gravity, pulling up the other car. The idea was not new: water-balanced lifts had been used at a number of different industrial sites in the 18th century – for example, at the iron works at Blaenafon – but the idea of using the system for tourists was very much a 19th-century notion. The Saltburn funicular railway opened in 1884 and, outwardly at least, very little has changed since then. One interesting difference, though, is that apparently we've all got a good deal bigger: whereas the cars could take 12 passengers when it opened, they now only hold a maximum of ten of

↖↑ The brakeman who controls the cars in his hut at the top of the slope *(left)*; buying tickets *(above)*.

PREVIOUS PAGES The Saltburn cliff lift – one carriage is going down balancing the other coming up.

us heftier modern citizens.

Passengers arriving at the bottom of the lift pass through the original iron turnstiles, still bearing the nameplates of their manufacturers, W Ellison & Son, into the hallway painted maroon and white – these just happen to be the colours used on the coaches of the North Eastern Railway, which took over the running of the local line. The attendant at the bottom communicates with the brakeman at the top. A single ring means everything's ready to go, which is then confirmed – but if a latecomer appears, three rings announce a short delay. The coaches are not the originals but closely resemble them. With their simple oak benches, they certainly look the part. For some reason, though, the

authorities decided several decades ago that the original Victorian stained-glass panels in the windows were old-fashioned and scrapped them. Rather belatedly, they realised that half the attraction of the railway was its nostalgic appeal, so a local stained-glass artist was called in to recreate them. Once the passengers are all aboard, the doors are shut and closed off from the outside, and the gates are shut. Sensors assure that everything is secure – if anything at all isn't right at the start or goes wrong during the short trip, automatic hydraulic brakes cut in. The ride may be dramatic up the 71% slope, but it is probably as safe as any transport system ever can be.

For the passengers, there is the pleasure of a gentle slow rise while the view down to the pier and out over the sea opens up. It all runs apparently effortlessly, but there is a lot of crafty Victorian engineering involved. A large tank at the bottom holds 36,000 gallons of water and another at the top holds 18,000 gallons, and each car has a tank underneath the passenger compartment that can hold 320 gallons. When a car reaches the bottom of the ride, it runs against a small projection that opens a valve in the water tank, allowing the water to run down a pipe into the main reservoir. At the top of the incline, the opposite occurs – the tank has to be filled with water. Obviously the top tank has to be topped up at regular intervals, and this is done by means of a pump at the bottom. The present pump, installed in 1974, replaces an earlier one powered by a gas engine, but this newer one is showing its age. At the time of writing, it was temporarily out of service and its job was being done by a modern submersible.

At the top of the slope, the brakeman has his little hut from which he controls the movement. Underneath the hut is the drum for the cables that are attached to the two cars. The brakeman operates a simple band brake – a wooden band that can be brought down onto the drum to stop it. The friction is so great that every morning he has to go down into the wheel pit to clear away the sawdust that has been rubbed off. The main control for the brake looks very like a ship's wheel. Everything here is about control – the speed of descent is limited, and the brakeman ensures that no one comes to a juddering stop at the end of the ride.

The joy of this little railway is its elegant simplicity – the only external power source it uses is for the pump. That very useful commodity called gravity does the rest. And this simple structure fits in perfectly with the seaside surroundings. They delighted the Victorians – and they are no less delightful today.

↗ The kiosk at the top of the lift.

→ The lower kiosk.

FABRICS

RUSH MATTING

No one really knows when the first rush floor mats were made, but there is archaeological evidence that they were in use in Mesopotamia around 6,000 years ago. There are no very early records in Britain, but we do know that rush mats were used in royal courts in the Tudor period and that their manufacture flourished in Southwark in South London at the time. What does seem fairly certain is that very little has changed in the way they have been made for centuries.

Rushmatters, based at a farm in the hamlet of Colesden in Bedfordshire, might never have existed but for a car accident in which a young woman named Felicity Irons was seriously injured. Unable to work during her recovery, she became bored and decided to learn a craft. She worked with both cane and rushes, but it was the rushes that appealed to her. She decided to set up her own business. Initially she obtained the rushes from an old rush cutter whose family had been engaged in the work for generations. When he died, she talked to his brother, who had no interest in taking over the business, but offered to show Felicity how the work was done. She had a two-hour lesson and that was it – she set up in business as a rush cutter as well as a rush weaver. And although the business has expanded over the years, this is the kernel of the whole operation – cutting the rushes, preparing them and using them, not just for floor matting but for a whole variety of different applications.

Anyone who thinks of rush weaving as being some sort of gentle craft has never seen the effort involved in harvesting the raw material. The rushes are obtained from the local rivers – the Bedfordshire Ouse, the Nene and the Ivel. The cutting season lasts for just five weeks in the summer and the working day starts as early as seven in the morning. The cutters go out armed with special knives with long handles and curved scythe-like blades. They use punts, and if water levels are high, they cut from these, but if levels are low they wade out to do the actual cutting and only use the punts for transport.

the main carpet, the plaits are 3 inches wide, and they are what is known as nine end flat weaves. In other words, nine individual strands are plaited together. The result could be seen in the workshop, where the plait looked like a long, coiled rope. One of Felicity's assistants, Adam, was busy sewing the 3-inch strips together using three-ply jute thread. To finish the mat, an edging is added, using a fine 11-end plait, just 1½ inches wide. But mats are by no means the only things produced here. In the next workshop, Felicity and her other assistant, Demi, were busy working on a variety of different products.

One of the projects on which Felicity was working was rush seating for a beautifully designed wooden-framed chair. What is notable is the delicacy of the workmanship. This process is weaving, as opposed to plaiting, and because a natural product is used, the subtle differences in shades and texture are endless. Demi, meanwhile, was weaving a cylindrical lidded basket, specially designed to house a set of rush tablemats. In order to work the rushes, they have to be moistened – the dry rushes are simply too brittle. Then it is a case of intricately weaving them in and out. There is a huge contrast between the hard, physical labour of rush cutting and the delicate work of weaving. The range that is produced is remarkably wide – there are the more obvious objects such as baskets and boxes, but also, more surprisingly, hats and even a pair of rush shoes. As with the mats, everything is made to order for specific clients and it does seem there is very little that Felicity and her team cannot make out of a humble plant growing in the local rivers.

This is strenuous work, as the cutters have to bend low to cut the plants just above the roots. This is an entirely sustainable harvest. The rushes start growing again immediately and an area that has been cut will be left to develop for at least two years before it is used again. Cutting the rushes helps to prevent them developing too much and clogging the waterways. But, at the same time, the plants themselves form a valuable part of the whole river system: they filter out pollutants and emit oxygen, which helps keep the river aerated and healthy.

Once the cutting is finished, the work has not yet ended. The rushes have to be taken back to the farm, where they are stacked against a long hedge to dry. On an average day, some two tons of rushes will be cut, but on drying they will lose up to 90% of that weight. Ideally they will continue the drying process in the open air, but, given the British climate, a suitable spell of sunny

↑ Loading rushes into the boat.

→ Cutting the rushes, tying them into bundles and carrying them ashore for storage.

PREVIOUS PAGES Felicity Irons cutting rushes.

....

weather cannot be guaranteed, and the process has to be completed in glasshouses. Felicity describes this period as like running a marathon a day. The dried rushes are stacked in one of two barns. The smaller of the pair is a fairly ordinary building, but the big barn is a truly spectacular medieval structure. As soon as the crop is in, the work of weaving and mat making can begin.

The core business has always been making floor mats. There are no standard mats – each one is created to the exact measurements provided by the client. The process starts by creating a plait, work that is done by locals in their own homes. For

....

OVERLEAF The magnificent medieval barn where the rushes are stored *(left)*. Weaving a seat for an elaborate wooden chair *(right)*.

THE HORSEHAIR MILL

Castle Cary in Somerset has been involved with textiles since at least the Middle Ages. It was originally a wool town, but with the decline of the wool trade in the west of England, manufacturers had to turn to other materials.

Flax was grown locally and was used for various products from sailcloth to twine, and hemp was used to make ropes. The town also lay at the heart of a prosperous agricultural region in which all the work on the farms relied on heavy horses. It was customary for the horses' tails to be cropped. Unlike docking, this is a harmless process, not really different from humans having their hair cut, except that it takes place at the opposite end of the animal. And, like human hair, the horses' tail hairs grow again. So there was a ready source of a useful raw material that could be woven to create a very durable fabric, while shorter hairs could be used for stuffing objects such as mattresses – they have the useful attribute that, having been sat on and squashed, they spring back again as soon as the load is removed. By the early 19th century, horsehair weaving had become firmly established in Castle Cary, and by 1831 there were two men and 24 women and children employed in weaving on handlooms there. This was the situation when the Scotsman John Boyd settled in the town and began manufacturing with horsehair in 1837.

Boyd was born in Old Cumnock in Ayrshire, probably in 1815, and with few opportunities there for an ambitious boy, his family found him a job as a travelling draper in Wincanton. His journeying would have taken him regularly to nearby Castle Cary, where he saw the opportunity to go into business for himself. His enterprise expanded and prospered, but still relied on weavers working on handlooms in their own homes. Most fabrics are woven in a very similar way. One set of threads, the warp, is wound onto a roller at the back of the loom and passed through looped wires, which form a heddle. The heddle can be raised and lowered alternately, leaving a space, the

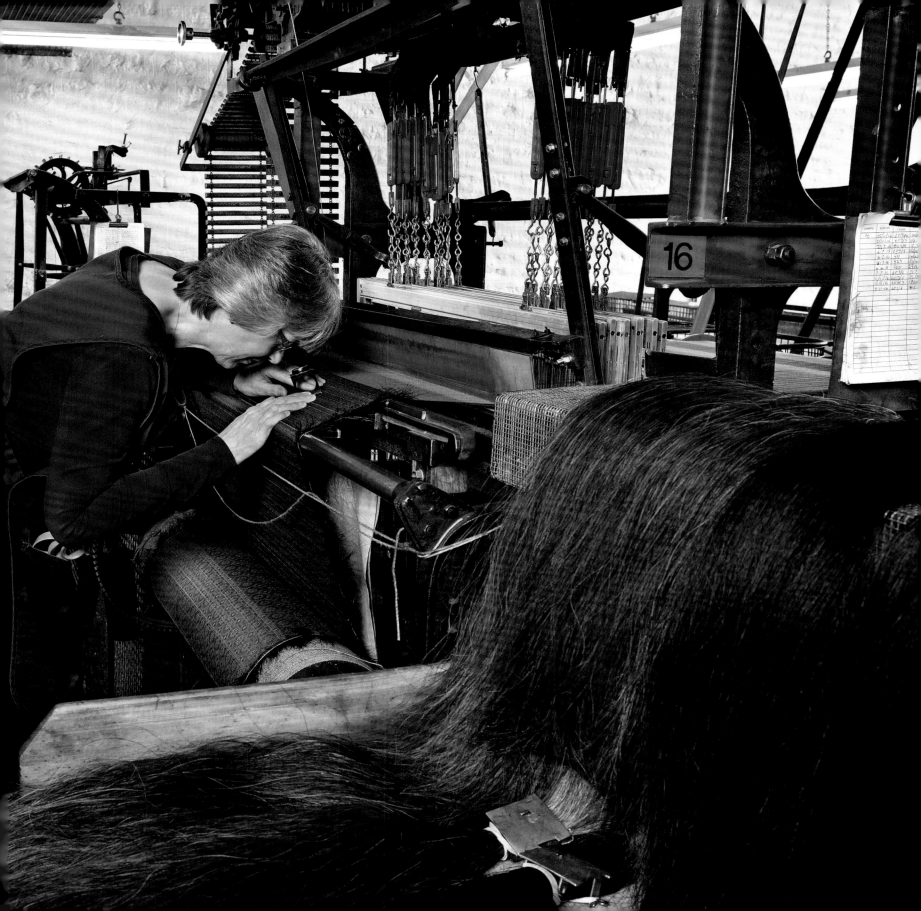

shed, through which the weft thread held in a shuttle can be passed. After each pass, the thread is beaten into place, then the shuttle is passed back again in the opposite direction. The threads themselves would be spun together to create a continuous, long yarn. Horsehair, however, is different. It is not spun. Warp threads have to be long, stretching round the roller and across the loom, so in horsehair weaving they have to come from some form of spun material; cotton is most commonly used, but linen thread is also employed, and for a really deluxe product the warp is silk. The weft, being horsehair, can't be put into a shuttle, so instead each individual hair has to be set in place, beaten down and the process repeated. This was very labour intensive, requiring a weaver and a helper, invariably a child, to keep up the supply of individual hairs.

John Boyd was not happy with the quality of hand-woven horsehair, but the impetus to make a major change came from an Act of Parliament of 1870 that made it compulsory for children to attend school up to the age of 12. This meant that Boyd would lose half his workforce, and employing two adults for each loom would have been decidedly uneconomical. He took the decision that the work would have to be mechanised. Power looms were already well established in the textile industry, but not adapted to the special needs of horsehair. So Boyd employed three men to work on developing a new loom – William Henderson, Henry Perkins, a blacksmith, and Joseph Chapman, a qualified mechanic. They were successful and Boyd was

↖← Heckling horsehair – removing short and broken hairs – at the John Boyd Mill *(above left)*; pressing finished cloth *(left)*.

PREVIOUS PAGES Checking the woven fabric for faults on the special horsehair loom.

able to patent the invention in 1872. He then set men to work building looms for the mill, which he now used for manufacture. It was said that he was impatient at the slow rate of progress in supplying the looms, which he put down to the locals' habit of consuming strong cider. Amazingly, however, 30 of those original looms are still at work at John Boyd Ltd, and if the founder were to come back today, although he would see some changes, everything would be very familiar. However, the power source for the looms has changed from the original water wheel, first to a steam engine and then to electricity.

In the 1950s, the company moved to a former flax mill, still in Castle Cary. The looms have not changed, though, and they are still powered by overhead line shafting and belts, just as they have been through all the changes, for the very good reason that they were built for this type of transmission and this is how they work at their best. There have been a lot of repairs, which is hardly surprising in machines that have long since passed their centenary, but there's no sending away for spare parts. These machines are unique, so anything that's

needed is made in the mill workshops, apart from new gears, which are cast in a nearby foundry. The Boyd mill is a typical 19th-century handsome set of stone buildings with iron-framed windows, and walking inside today really is walking into history.

Horses no longer work the surrounding fields, so the hair is imported from Mongolia and Siberia via China. This is the natural horsehair, cropped from working horses – and it has to come from live animals. The first stage in the procedure is to dye the hair. The work is done at the mill, where specific colours can be created in the mill's own lab to meet a client's specification. The dyes are all made from animal protein. Hairs to be dyed black, for example, are heated in the vat at 90ºC for four hours and then hung up to dry; if other colours are used, the hair is dried laid out flat. The material used for the warp threads is dyed by a company in Huddersfield.

The hair is not yet ready for weaving, though. The next stage is hackling. The bunch of hairs is drawn through a series of tall spikes to remove any short or broken hairs: it is essential for the weaving process that they are all the same length. This hackling process

will be repeated several times before the work is completed. And now, before the hair can be used it has to be closely inspected to make sure that every single hair in the bundle is the same colour as all the rest.

In the meantime, the warp will be prepared, using whichever thread is appropriate – normally cotton. The cones of coloured yarn are set on a frame, then run through a wire grid to align them in the correct order – they might, for example, be required to be in alternating stripes for a patterned fabric. Then they are wound onto a large drum so that they form a close web of threads exactly the width required for the finished fabric. This width is determined by the length of the hair: no fabric can be wider than the hair length, usually between 22 and 24 inches. Once one band of warp thread is complete, the mechanism moves along the drum and a second band can be created, and so on. When everything is in place, the yarn is transferred to a beam, a simple roller that is placed in the back of the loom, and the individual threads are passed through the heddle.

The 30 looms are spread over two floors, and the weaving rooms are places of noise and motion. There is a perpetual clatter from the constant movement of the rotating belts and the intricate actions of the machinery. After hackling, the hair is given a thorough combing before the actual weaving begins. At the side of each loom is a trough of water that contains two bunches of hair. This is automatically rocked backwards and forwards so that each bunch is presented in turn to the picker. The weaving process is absolutely fascinating to watch. The delicate movement of the picker is almost impossible to follow as it plucks out an individual hair. The actual design is a closely guarded secret, but basically it consists of no more than 10cm of steel wire acting as a tiny pair of tweezers. The motion of the rapier shuttle is altogether more obvious, activated by a large jointed iron arm that moves in and out like a snooker player's elbow when making a shot. Peering into the workings, one can only marvel at the intricate array of cams and gears that keep everything in precise coordination. These days, the greatest demand is for plain fabric, but some patterned fabric is still produced.

Patterns are produced on a special dobby loom. The name derives from an abbreviation of 'draw boy'. To create a pattern, it is necessary to lift different warp threads in a particular order: if, for example, the horsehair was white and the warp threads black, the pattern created would depend on which thread showed on the top surface. Lifting the threads in the right order was originally the job of the draw boy, who literally drew them up by hand in the correct order; in the dobby, however, a rotating chain mechanism on the end of the loom determines the order instead.

Removing the cloth from the loom is not the end of the process: it then has to

← Inspecting the dyed hair for faults before it is sent for weaving.

↑ Sir Edwin Lutyens at ease in his unusual chair.

....

be pressed, which both helps to compact the fibres and adds the sheen that is a characteristic of horsehair fabric. Lengths of fabric are packed between layers of cardboard and then made into multi-layered packages. Metal plates, heated in an oven, are then placed between the packages and piled up in the press. West Country readers looking at the photo of the process may think it looks rather familiar, which is not surprising, since it started its working life as a cider press. The actual pressure is provided by the capstan on top. A long metal bar is placed into a socket on a nut that engages with the screw to force the press down. The fabric is now ready to be despatched, and is lowered down by a manually operated hoist outside the building.

↑ A sample of 'Lutyens' cloth.

↑ 'Mackintosh' cloth.

John Boyd has provided textiles for some illustrious clients over the years, including two of Britain's most famous architects. Sir Edwin Lutyens is best known in Britain for Castle Drogo in Devon, a building that, while outwardly forbidding, has a comfortable domestic interior, and internationally for planning and designing the government buildings for the Indian capital, New Delhi. Lutyens saw a painting of Napoleon sitting in an asymmetric chair and had one made for himself and upholstered in Boyd horsehair. Charles Rennie Mackintosh was the country's finest exponent of the Art Nouveau movement, and the famous Willow Tearooms in Glasgow are still furnished with fabrics from Castle Cary. It is no surprise, then, to discover that modern interior designers have recognised the unique durability and beauty of horsehair cloth made in the same traditional way today by John Boyd as it was made when those two great architects placed their orders.

THE LACE MAKERS

When you are looking for a sense of historical continuity, it is very rare to find anywhere with material whose associations range from an invention from the reign of Elizabeth I to electronic machinery from the 21st century. Yet that is exactly what we found at the Shawl Factory, home to GH Hurt & Son. The story really begins in 1589 with the invention of the stocking frame.

Until that time, stockings had simply been knitted by hand. The man who invented a machine that would do the job instead was William Lee of Calverton in Nottinghamshire. Not a lot is known about Lee, but a great deal has been invented about him. He is usually referred to as a clergyman, though his name never appears in any church records. He is said to have invented his machine because his wife was too busy knitting to pay any attention to him, so he made a machine that would take the work away from her – which is one of those stories, like that of James Watt and the kettle, that some people seem to find essential to explain why an inventor had an idea, instead of crediting him with intelligence, application and foresight. What we do know is that he made the machine, with the help of his brother James, and it was very successful – too successful, as it turned out, as it was widely pirated and Lee never got the patent he needed to ensure he got his due rewards. In disgust, he moved to France, where he was no more successful in making money and died in poverty.

Lee's machine was complex, and the following description is very simplified. It consists of a massive frame, and the actual needles are fixed and end in hooks. The moving parts are metal plates, known as sinkers, placed between the needles. When these are lowered, they push thread down into a series of kinks that can be formed into loops. They do not move all at once, as that would strain the machine, but instead move one at a time, with the distinctive noise of the knitting frame, something like running a stick along iron railings. The sinkers now move forward, pushing the loop onto the hooks. If they continued moving forward, they would also push the loops onto the needles,

so Lee arranged for a separate metal plate, the presser bar, to push the needles' hooks down into grooves, closing them off. Now the presser bar is raised clear, and the threads can be pushed through the loops, creating the interlocking of a line of knitting. Now a new line of thread can be laid across and the whole process repeated. All this requires considerable coordination from the worker, who has to work with handles to either side of the frame and with foot treadles. It is also hard work, even though the effort is reduced thanks to overhead spring attachments.

For a long time, the stocking frame, as it came to be known, was worked by framework knitters in their own homes. Later, workshops were established, and in the early 19th century employers began to look for ways to cut costs. Legally, they were forced by an Act of Parliament only to use journeymen who had served a full apprenticeship, but more and more were taken on without the qualification. The framework knitters asked the authorities to intervene to enforce the law, but no one

took any notice. They then decided to take matters into their own hands: they began telling the employers that unless they complied with the law they would break the machines – and when that had no effect, they turned threat into action. To preserve anonymity, the machine breakers were led by the mythical General Ludd – hence they became known as Luddites. The authorities, who had previously shown little interest in the legal rights of the framework knitters, soon became far more active in putting down Luddism, with ferocious intensity. Life eventually settled back to normal and by the 1840s records showed that there were 16,382 stocking frames in use in the Nottingham area.

The early machines had knitted plain fabric, but it was soon recognised that by introducing eyelets into the process, loops could be moved from one needle to another, so that gaps would be left to create patterns in the stockings. From there it was only a short step to adapt the stocking frame to making lace. Which finally brings

↖ Pinning out a washed shawl to create a scalloped edge.

↑ A damp shawl being stacked in the drying room.

PREVIOUS PAGES Checking the quality of a lace shawl at GH Hurt & Son.

↓ Edging a shawl.

us to the Hurt family. George Henry Hurt began working in the hosiery business and became the manager of a shawl and hosiery company before deciding to set up in business for himself manufacturing Shetland shawls in Chigwell to the south of Nottingham. Once this had been an entirely rural area, famous for its apple orchards, but times were changing. Hurt bought a former seed warehouse, built around 1781, and brought in some old knitting frames and men to work them. The original building still stands, a narrow, two-storey brick structure with the telltale sack hoist and loading bays down one side. Chigwell itself has changed completely: no orchards exist now as it has been all but engulfed by housing spread out from the city. But inside the building there are still those old knitting frames bought by George Hurt, some of them at least two hundred years old. They have not been changed much over the years, but one had to be given a new frame two centuries after having been burned in the Luddite uprising.

Two of the old frames are still regularly used. Henry Hurt, grandson of the founder, joined the company in 1953 at the age of 18 and served a six-month apprenticeship on the knitting machines, and he still demonstrates them today, when the firm opens its doors to visitors. But these machines still have the potential to be much more than museum pieces. A student, Jacaranda Brain, has arrived on a job placement and is learning the complexities of knitting lace on the handframes. Henry's daughter, Gillian Taylor, the member of the next generation to join the family firm, feels that if they can develop new designs for scarves on the old machines they will find a niche market in the burgeoning heritage industry. How satisfying it would be to find a machine basically designed over four hundred years ago and built two hundred years ago still finding its place in the commercial world of the 21st century! There is, of course, one small problem: no one is making spares for two-hundred-year-old

....

↓ ↘ A finished shawl *(below)*; a Hurt's shawl was used to wrap the latest addition to the Royal Family *(bottom right)*.

machines. The sinkers are complex pieces of metal, and they differ from one machine to the next. Fortunately, however, there are still moulds available from which new sinkers can be cast using molten lead.

But a business cannot survive on nostalgia, and Henry Hurt started introducing more modern machinery in the 1950s. First were the mechanical flat bed knitting machines. These are automatic, with the pattern controlled by punched cards that determine which needles are in use for each row of knitting. Again, this is not exactly a new concept. The French inventor Joseph Marie Jacquard was the first to develop the punched-card system for automating ornate patterns on looms in the silk industry in 1801. These machines are now more or less obsolete – they cannot be expected to remain in use as long as the old handframes, and one has been taken out of service to be cannibalised for spares. The most modern machines in the workshop are electronic, computer controlled and far more versatile. While the older ones could do only plain knitting, the new ones can both knit and purl.

So a new range of products has been added – baby hats and mittens in cashmere. But the Shetland shawl remains at the heart of what they do at GH Hurt & Son.

When work began using the oldest machines, there was a particular problem to overcome: the traditional shawl has a plain centre but a decorative border, and because the machine can knit but not purl, the border and centre had to be made separately. The two parts were then sent out to workers in nearby cottages to be sewn together. This is no longer the case with modern machines. But even after knitting, there are more processes to go through. The shawl will have a serrated margin, which is produced just as it was when the pattern originated in Shetland. The shawl is washed and then attached to a frame. The frame itself is slightly bigger than the shawl and has rows of pins all round the edge. The threads have to be pulled outwards to fit over the pins, creating the scalloped effect. The material is then taken off to the drying room. Originally, this had a small furnace in the centre, but today it has banks of radiators all round the walls, keeping the room uncomfortably hot: not a place to linger even on a chilly day.

The margin of the shawl is not just scalloped, it is also given a raised decoration, rather like rows of miniature cushions, using the shell edging machine. This was bought second-hand in the 1950s and was certainly not very new then: the American manufacturer had been making them since the 1890s. There is a more modern and more expensive version, but it rarely gets used. It's simply not as good as its aged companion. One of the features we have found when looking at traditional industries is that this often seems to be the case: the old outperforms the modern. On three occasions during the manufacturing process the shawl

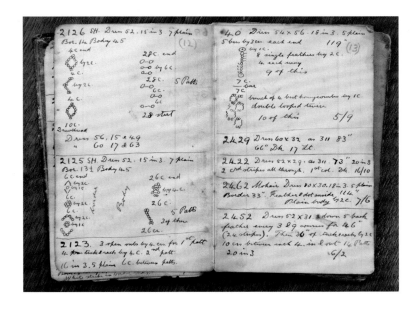

← Jacaranda Brain and Henry Hurt at work on two of the very old knitting frames.

→ An old pattern book.

is inspected for faults. When any are found they are corrected by hand. This is delicate work that requires intimate knowledge of the different stitches needed and dextrous skill. The main instrument used looks like a thin bodkin, but look closer at the metal spike and you can just about make out the tiny hook at the end. The final machine in the line is used for overlocking, closing off the edges of the shawl. Then, threaded with ribbon, it is ready to be worn. The baby shawl is a truly beautiful garment, light yet cosily warm. There was a time, however, when it seemed to be going out of fashion. Then Prince William and the Duchess of Cambridge had a baby and they were photographed leaving the hospital with the infant wrapped in a shawl. A gust of wind caught the corner of the shawl and revealed the maker's mark – and the name of GH Hurt appeared on front pages around the world. Suddenly, the order books had never been fuller.

Hurt's is a family firm, with Gillian Taylor the fourth generation to join the company. But it is not only the members of the Hurt

family who span the generations there. Reg Robbins' mother and grandmother both worked for the firm, and his own career has seen him coping with all the changes. Now employed as the hand knitting mechanic in charge of all the knitting machines, he began just as everyone there did, by working on the hand machines when he arrived as a 16-year-old apprentice back in 1971. Irene Wilson is also a long-serving member of staff, and when her daughter Jayne joined as well and ended up marrying Reg, she added to the Robbins family connection. This sense of continuity permeates everything about the factory and the work, from machines staying in use when all commercial logic suggests they should have been scrapped about a hundred years ago, to members of the same family following each other into the factory. The result is not just a product of which any manufacturer would be proud, but I don't recall ever having been to a workplace where people seemed more cheerful and happy with what they were doing. That is a tradition that also looks like continuing for a long time to come.

HARRIS TWEED

At a recent event someone commented on my smart new jacket; smart it may have been, but new it certainly was not. I had bought it nearly 30 years ago, but it still showed little signs of age, unlike its owner. That was, of course, because it was made out of a very special, attractive and hard-wearing cloth – Harris tweed.

The word 'tweed' first appeared in 1826, when a London clerk misread the label on a batch of 'tweel' from Hawick in the Scottish Borders. He assumed the name derived from the Scottish river – even though Hawick is not on the Tweed. In fact tweel was a type of cloth then popular for travelling cloaks. Somehow or other the name seemed appropriately Scottish anyway so it was kept. It was not a name limited to any one part of Scotland.

The Outer Hebrides were, like many other Scottish regions, largely self-sufficient. Cloth was produced by the crofters from their own sheep, and they would spin, card, weave and finish it in their own homes. It was a strong, durable material suitable for the often harsh weather conditions of the islands. Life in the Hebrides continued in its traditional patterns for centuries, with crofters tilling the land and fishing. But in the 1840s a serious problem arose: a blight destroyed the potato crop, a staple diet for the islanders. The blight is best known for its effect in bringing starvation to Ireland, but it was scarcely less devastating in the Hebrides. Lady Dunmore, the widow of Lord Dunmore, whose family owned most of Harris, felt that something needed to be done to bring in a new income. She ordered a tweed in the family's clan tartan and showed it off to her wealthy friends. This created a demand for Harris tweed and brought much short-term relief but, more importantly, established a long-term industry.

The success of Harris tweed encouraged others to copy the cloth and use the name as a selling point – even if the cloth had not been made in the Hebrides and, in some cases, not even in Scotland at all. It was decided to gain protection for the true cloth by establishing a legal definition. The Harris Tweed Association Ltd was established in 1906, and in 1909 the Harris trademark consisting of an orb topped

with a Maltese cross was legally established. Over the years the definition of how cloth had to be made was changed from an initial condition that allowed yarn from any Scottish mill to be used to the more limited criteria in force today. Harris tweed has to be made from pure Scottish wool and all the processing, from carding and spinning to finishing, has to be carried out in the Hebrides. Most of these processes now take place in mills on the islands, but weaving still has to be done on handlooms in the islanders' own homes. There was a move to take weaving into the mills as well, using fast, modern machinery, but the weavers almost unanimously rejected the proposal.

The initial processes of turning the wool from the sheep into cloth are basically the same as for other woollen cloths, but with a few very special characteristics. Once the wool has been cleaned it is dyed in batches using only natural dyes. These produce soft colours reminiscent of the landscape and seascape of the islands. The different batches are then thoroughly mixed in exactly determined proportions before spinning.

The result is a very strong thread that is no one specific colour but a blend. It is not uniform, which means that the resulting cloth will have a wonderful texture and a very natural-seeming colour: it will never be harsh or gaudy. The yarn is now supplied to the weavers in one of two forms.

All weaving depends on two lots of yarn. One set, the warp, is fixed in the loom. To put it at its simplest, the warp threads are taken from bobbins on a warping frame and then wound onto a roller, usually known as a beam, in a specific order if they are to form part of a pattern. They are fitted closely together, and the number of these threads will determine the eventual width of the cloth. Warping usually takes place in the mill, and the beam is then sent across to the weaver, who will attach it to the back of the loom. Setting up the warp threads is a complex operation, but the essential part is that each thread will pass through an eyelet in a set of wires known as a heddle. The heddle can be alternately raised and lowered, creating a gap through which the weft thread can be passed. This setting in place of all the warp thread has to be completed before weaving can start.

The weft thread arrives on bobbins and has to be wound onto the spindle in the shuttle. When the warp threads are raised and lowered, a space – the shed – is left, through which the shuttle can be passed, trailing its thread behind it. This is then firmly bound into place, ready for the shuttle to be returned in the opposite direction. Originally the shuttle was thrown by hand and the heddle raised and lowered by means of foot treadles. The system was improved in the 18th century by the introduction of the flying shuttle, which enabled the weaver to jerk a handle to activate artificial arms

at each side of the loom. The shuttle was fitted with wheels and ran rapidly across a wooden board – hence the name 'flying shuttle'. By the early 19th century, the whole system was adapted by using a system of gears and levers so that all the operations could be automated, with power provided originally by a water wheel, later by a steam engine and in modern times by an electric motor. The handloom had become a power loom. This meant that the weaving could be taken out of the homes and done in the mills instead. This happened in the major production centres of mainland Britain, but not in the Hebrides. But there was one change that did affect the islands.

The story begins in Yorkshire with the firm of George Hattersley & Sons, which established a factory in Keighley in the early 19th century. It was the son who first designed a power loom for weaving worsted cloth. The power loom was a success and he went on to develop the dobby loom that enabled more complex patterns to be woven. So far, the looms had all been intended for use in mills, but Hattersley went on to design a domestic loom. This worked in exactly the same way that a mill loom worked, except that instead of being powered by steam or water, the

power came from the weaver himself via a foot treadle. In 1919 thirty of these looms were sent to the islands, where they became an instant success. An improvement came in 1924 with the six-shuttle loom. Each shuttle could carry a different-coloured thread and could be brought into play as required to create any particular pattern. Over a century later, these looms are still in use.

The tradition of weaving with the Hattersley domestic loom not only lives on, but seems to have produced a hardy brand of weaver. Pedalling the loom all day long must be rather like going to the gym for several hours a day. Joe MacDonald, who still weaves in his workshop in a converted garage, is 87 years old. His friend Chris Anderson, seen with him on page 141, is a youthful 74. If there is any shadow hanging over this traditional industry, it is the question of how many young people will want to keep it going. There is no denying the fact that the domestic loom is an anachronism and that the same quality could almost certainly be produced on a loom powered by electricity rather than foot power. But of course the weavers of Harris and Lewis would dispute this, and they can at least point to the fact that even if, which they think unlikely, the power loom could produce cloth of equal quality, it will never produce anything of a better quality.

← The cluttered workshop – the most obvious piece of machinery is used to wind the yarn onto a spindle for the shuttle.

↗ The loom is worked by pedalling all day on a foot treadle.

PREVIOUS PAGES Joe McDonald at his loom with his friend Chris Andrews.

SPORTS AND GAMES

THE FOOTBALL MATCH

Walking from the outskirts of Ashbourne in Derbyshire into the centre of town on a damp, dark, cold Tuesday morning was rather like walking into a ghost town or one preparing for a siege. The shops were all closed, and frontages were boarded up, protected by stout wooden planks. The town was not preparing for war, just for a football match – but this was to be a football match unlike any other. For this was the day before Royal Ash Wednesday, and on that afternoon mayhem would break out in the streets of this attractive market town.

What sets this football match apart, for a start, is that the ball is rarely kicked. The distance between the 'goals' is not measured in yards: they are three miles apart, and rather than just 11 players on each team, or even 15, the numbers are unlimited. Rules are few, but the first of them gives an idea of what lies ahead: 'Committing murder or manslaughter is prohibited.'

The objective of the game is easily explained. There are two teams, the Up'ards and the Down'ards, and which one you belong to as a native of Ashbourne depends on which side of the river you live on. The aim is to carry the ball to the goal on your own side, which, in the case of the Up'ards, is a plinth on the site of Clifton Mill, and for the Down'ards it is one at the former Sturston Mill. To score a goal, it is necessary to tap the ball on the goal three times. And that basically is it, with play for the day starting at 2pm – and allowed to go on until 10 at night. What is involved in getting the ball to the goal becomes clearer once the game gets under way. Almost anything is allowed, though the second rule does state: 'Unnecessary violence is frowned on' – not, one notices, actually disallowed. One local remarked: 'It's a great day for settling scores, even with someone on your own side.' There is certainly something satisfying about seeing a game that has

been played in Britain for over a thousand years, and if it seems a bit quirky, whoever said there was anything wrong with that? No one really knows how long the game has been played in Ashbourne, as most records were lost in a fire in the 19th century, but documents do go back to the 17th century and indicate that it was considered ancient even then. What is so incredible about this sport is the ebullience and enthusiasm that has kept it going through the centuries. This is no half-hearted reenactment of some ancient tradition, but an event that is taken seriously, and the game is played and supported with as much enthusiasm as any national cup final.

If the outskirts of Ashbourne were all but deserted, the centre around the market square was already crowded by midday. Unlike the shops, the pubs were very much open for business, packed inside and with customers spilling out into the street. But as two o'clock approached, the crowds began to make their way to the start, the main town car park, emptied of vehicles for the day. A brick plinth at the centre, boasting a pair of Union Jacks, was the focal point and it was from here that the 'turner-up' would start the game, by throwing the ball into the heart of the waiting crowd. The ball itself is slightly bigger than a regulation football and made of cork, for the very good reason that it is certain to spend a lot of time bobbing about in water. The turner-up is chosen for each game and has the honour of deciding just how the ball is going to be decorated, after which a local artist is given the task of painting it. The end result looks a bit like a colourful beach ball, but there the resemblance to any game ever played on a beach ends.

Before play starts there are a few simple announcements, reminding players to keep out of certain areas, such as churchyards, and gently pointing out to spectators that

← ↑ Once the ball has been thrown into the crowd, the wrestling competitors go through streams and crowd the town streets as they try to reach one of the goals.

PREVIOUS PAGES The Royal Shrove Tuesday football match at Ashbourne – competitors fight for the ball in the pond.

if the stewards tell them to move, they'd be well advised to do so, or risk being trampled. Then the crowd is invited to sing 'Auld Lang Syne' followed by the National Anthem, a reminder that this game does indeed have royal patronage. After this, the ball is turned up – thrown into the crowd. What a moment before had been several thousand people standing around singing suddenly becomes a human tsunami as the players and ball surge down towards the river, the crowd following in their wake. To the uninitiated, which certainly included myself, it all seems confusion. The ball itself is invisible, lost in the heaving crowd of players. But you soon realise that there is a lot going on and the position of the ball is

obvious, as players literally climb over each other to get their hands on it. Yet, in spite of all the shoving and heaving, nothing seems to move and a cloud of steam rises above the scene as the players do their best to create some movement. Then, quite unexpectedly, the ball appears above the throng and the watching crowd surge along with the rapidly moving bunch around the ball. The movement may not be great, but it takes the players first down into the river, then out again and onto the banks of the lake in the park. Inevitably, it seems, for it always happens, the ball rises from the throng and ends up in the lake. You might expect some kind soul to fish it out and put it back in play. But that's not the way they play here. Men hurl themselves into the water, fighting to get their hands on the ball. And what had looked like an oversized rugby scrum now briefly turns into something more like water polo. Then it is out of the water again, and the pushing and tugging, hauling and heaving continues. Out of the river and out of the park, everyone moves

into the streets of the town, and now it is all too clear why everywhere is boarded up – and why we were advised not to park the car anywhere near the centre.

At some stage one player will have been appointed by each team to be the scorer. As the situation becomes more fluid and all the action is moving one way, there are shouts from one section of the crowd of 'Down wi' it!' They can see that the opposition is getting the upper hand so want the ball grounded to stop the progress. But as it moves backwards through one section, the time has come for runners to start making real progress. Eventually, after hours of battling, the Up'ards scored at nearly half past eight in the evening. And that was it – the game was over – but the celebrations certainly were not. There were probably nuances and subtleties lost on me but obvious to the passionately involved local community. But even without understanding everything that happened that day it was still a remarkable experience, and heartening to find that this very ancient game is played with as much vigour today as it has been for centuries. It was a unique experience, and made watching a rugby international at Twickenham seem positively sedate by comparison.

← Each year the honour of choosing the design for the ball goes to a different citizen of the town.

↑ One of the two stones at either end of the course that has to be touched by the ball to score a goal.

REAL TENNIS

Anyone visiting Jesmond Dene in Newcastle-upon-Tyne might come across an ornate red brick building and wonder what it was – a nonconformist chapel perhaps? It is highly unlikely that, if they didn't know already, they would guess its true function. For this is a tennis court – not for playing the sort of match one sees at Wimbledon, but one built for the far older game of real, or royal, tennis.

Real tennis has a long and complex history, elements of which can often seem quite tenuous. According to some authorities it began as a form of handball, played against the wall in ancient Greece and Rome. The Romans introduced it to Gaul, and there it became more sophisticated. Gloves were used and improved by the addition of gut strings, providing greater impetus to the ball. This eventually led to the strings being stretched across a frame with a handle – and the tennis racquet was born. Further changes came when, instead of simply hitting the ball against a wall and returning it – as in fives and squash – the game was played in a closed room with a net down the middle, and with opponents facing each other. It was very popular from the medieval period onwards, often played in abbeys and monasteries, and later became a popular game with aristocrats and even royalty – hence royal tennis. Shakespeare has Henry V – who, as the young Prince Hal, had a notably dissolute lifestyle – being sent a set of tennis balls from France as a taunting present. But it has to be said that Shakespeare is not perhaps a stickler for historical accuracy. What we do know is that one of the most enthusiastic players of the game was Henry VIII, who was generally considered one of the finest in the country. On the other hand, it would have been a very bold courtier who thought it a good idea to beat the king: losing a game is always better than losing a head. Over time, the courts became more or less standardised and sets of rules were laid down, which are the ones followed in the modern game.

Courts come in two basic types, but the one most commonly used in Britain is the one we find at Jesmond Dene, built in 1894. Inside

↑ There are many ways of scoring points – one is to hit the ball into this area, ringing the bell.

PREVIOUS PAGES A match in progress at the Jesmond Dene Real Tennis Club.

is the enclosed court itself, rather larger than a lawn tennis court, but what is most striking about its appearance is the addition of the structures within the playing area. On three sides of the court, there are areas with sloping roofs, known as penthouses. All the serving is done from one end of the court; the penthouse at that end is the dedans, the one at the opposite end the grille. Stretching down the length of the court is the side penthouse on the server's side of the net, and the service penthouse at the other. There are galleries under the penthouses that also have a part to play in the game. The floor is marked out in a series of lines, with a rectangular area at the receiver's end – the receiving court. As one can imagine, the complexity of the court is reflected in equally arcane rules.

The server has to hit the ball so that it touches the side penthouse and bounces in the receiving court. The score goes up in 15s as in lawn tennis, but there are lots of differences in play. In real tennis, it is acceptable for the ball to bounce twice, and what follows is a chase – the ball can be returned, and it counts as long as the return lands further away from the net on the far side than the distance from the net

↓ The club building.

↗→ A doubles match at Jesmond Dene *(above right)*; the club room *(right)*.

Then another turn round is made between the first, and so on until the entire ball is rigidly held together in a string nest. The next stage is to wrap it tightly in tape, and hammer it firmly in place to create a round ball. This core will last for a long time. The final stage is to add the outer covering, made from specially woven cloth. It resembles and is very like a conventional tennis ball cover. This is tacked into place, then sewn together and the tacks removed. The cover does not last as long as the core, so is regularly replaced.

It is not difficult to see why several people thought this old game just too complicated for its own good, and simplified the rules to create the modern game of lawn tennis, which also has the advantage that you don't have to build an expensive and complex building in order to start playing. On the other hand, there is something irresistible about a sport that has survived down the centuries, however odd it might be.

↑→ The receiving end of the court *(above)* and the serving end *(opposite)*.

↓ The various stages in making a real tennis ball.

where it bounced. There are other ways of scoring points – for example, by hitting the ball directly into certain areas of the galleries beneath the penthouses. As in squash, the same player continues serving until a point is lost, at which point the players change ends. There are other rules, which make sense when the game is being played, but for the reader that is probably quite enough to get some idea of just what a game of real tennis involves. It is a bit like a combination of lawn tennis and squash and more complicated than either – but just as energetic.

There are only a couple of dozen real tennis courts in Britain. So it is no surprise to find that there is only one manufacturer of the special, slightly oblong-headed racquets in Britain – and that no one makes the balls. The clubs therefore have no option – they have to make their own. The process starts by crushing up old corks to form the core of the ball – so it helps to have a good supply of wine drinkers in the club. This is then

wrapped in material, usually a discarded cover from an old ball, and this is then bound by thin cord. One end of the cord is fastened around a vertical post so that the other end can be kept taut. It is wound round the cloth once, then the ball is turned and a second winding is made at right angles to the first.

THE HIGHLAND GAMES

Tradition has it that these games have their origin in one of the oldest sporting events ever held in the British Isles. The story goes that King Malcolm III of Scotland (r.1058–1093) called on strong, fast runners to turn up at some meadows, known then as Brae O'Mar (modern Braemar), where they would race each other up Craig Choinnich and back. The winners would then be appointed as the king's messengers.

Later, it seems, different contests were held between members of the various clans, tests not only of physical prowess but also of music and dancing ability. These two facets of the games have continued into the modern era. But the games were brought to a sudden halt with the defeat of the 1745 Highland uprising in support of Bonnie Prince Charlie. Punitive measures were introduced, including a ban on the wearing of the kilt, the playing of bagpipes and any large gatherings of Highlanders. It was only after the repeal of these laws that Highland Societies were formed, and a Clan Gathering was held at Falkirk in 1781. But it was the 19th century that saw the introduction of the traditional elements that make up the modern Games. History also played a part in their spread around the world. The infamous Highland Clearances saw many Scots forced off the land, and huge numbers emigrated, and wherever they settled, whether in Canada or across the world in Australia, they took their old customs with them, including the Games.

The North Berwick Games take place in the local recreation ground under the shapely cone of the volcanic hill known as the Law. In 2017, these Games hosted an international pipe band competition, with bands arriving from around the world – more than 80 of them altogether, so that wherever you went, the sound of drums and pipes went with you. Outside the arena, bands would be tuning up and practising, while inside were two performance areas, each with three

judges, covering the two different categories: the local Lothian and Borders competition and the Open. Within these two broad groups was everything from children's bands to the most experienced. Even though I knew that this was an international competition, it still came as a surprise to hear the announcement that the next band to appear would be from Omaha, Nebraska. And in they marched in their kilts and Highland dress. Each band marches in, the pipe major shakes hands with a judge, and then they march smartly before wheeling to form a circle and performing their set pieces. One judge is only concerned with their deportment, how smartly they march in, how coordinated they are in their performance; the second judges the pipes and the third the drums. The drumming is quite distinctive: there are the snare drums, played with hard sticks; the tenor drums, which have drumsticks with soft heads that are extravagantly flourished and whirled; and the bass drum. It has to be confessed that for an uninitiated Englishman it is virtually impossible to tell which is the best, but enthusiasts permanently occupy the grandstand by the arena next to one of the performance areas.

The other feature on the musical side is the dancing. Again, it is hard to distinguish the best, but at least one can see that some performers move with more grace and a better sense of timing with the music than others. It is also obvious that this is a difficult art that requires quite a high degree of athletic ability as well as musical sensibility. And they start at a very young age – some of the competitors were obviously still at primary school. Music and dance are clearly a vital part of the Games, even if it is difficult to think of them as competitive sports. However, the events that get under way in the afternoon most definitely fall into this

category. They are known as the 'heavy events' – a term that is as applicable to the various objects being thrown as it is to most of the competitors.

There are events in the programme that seem familiar – events you might expect to find at any athletics meeting, such as putting the shot and throwing the hammer. The former is, indeed, very much what you would

....

←↓ Throwing the hammer *(opposite);* a unique event – throwing the boulder *(below).*

expect. But the hammer is significantly different. In modern athletics, the hammer is a metal ball on the end of a chain with a handle and the throwers pirouette to gain momentum before letting the missile loose. Here, the hammer is much more obviously a successor to the sledgehammers that were supposed to have been used when the event was first staged. There is still a metal ball, but now it is stuck on the end of a long stick; and instead of spinning him or herself round, the competitor whirls it round his or her head

Finally in the heavy event section came that peculiarly Scottish sport, tossing the caber. The caber itself is a long, heavy lump of wood, originally a tree trunk, which the competitors have to lift into their cupped hands and hoist into a vertical position resting on the shoulder. Once the caber is settled in place, they begin to run forward and, once they have their momentum going, hurl it high into the air. Unlike the other throwing events, distance is immaterial. For a throw to be good, the caber has to fall away from the thrower; if it topples backwards, it doesn't count. The throw is then judged on straightness. If one thinks of the thrower standing at number six on a clock dial, then the caber should be pointing straight at the twelve. It is apparently very rare for this to be achieved. It looks horrendously difficult, and it was made even worse that afternoon when, just as the first few throws had been completed, the heavens opened up. Keeping hold of a dry caber looks tough enough; handling a soaking wet one must be far worse. Needless to say, perhaps, no one seemed deterred. They obviously produce a tough breed of men and women in the Highlands.

The Games are sometime dismissed as a Victorian invention – even by native Scots – and that may be so. But there is no doubt that they are firmly established, are hugely popular with the crowds and have a unique character. And in a sporting era where money seems to rule, it is good to come to an event with such a good spirit. Even the losers looked as if they were enjoying every minute just as much as the winners – and that's a rare but welcome sight. And even a visiting Englishman who can't tell a march from a strathspey came away with a smile on his face – even if it was a rather wet one.

– and, yes, women do take part, including Laura, who had come from Switzerland specially for the Games. Then comes a variation of the shot put: putting the stane – which is a Scottish stone, except that it's more like a giant boulder weighing around half a hundredweight. The ungainly rock makes throwing doubly difficult: it's hard to get a good grip on it, and it is very definitely not aerodynamically helpful. The next heavy event involved hurling a weight over a bar. It is again said to have had specific local origins, in this case dating back to the time when crofters regularly threw bales of hay up into the hayloft. There is a 56lb weight for the men and a 26lb one for the women. The competitor has to stand with their back to

↑ The women's hammer competition.

→ The Highland Dance competition for young girls. *(opposite top right)*; tossing the caber *(opposite below)*.

the bar and is only allowed to use one hand. The trick is to start it swinging between the legs then hurl it back over the head and, with luck, over the bar. The competition started with the bar at a daunting 11 feet from the ground and went up a foot at a time until there was a winner. What was really noticeable and, one suspects, typical of the Games is the fact that although there is obvious rivalry and a will to win, everyone encourages each other. These could be renamed the Good-Natured Games.

BALLOONS

History records many doomed accounts of humans attempting to fly, usually by strapping wings to their backs, then jumping off high buildings flapping furiously and ending up with, at best, broken bones. Then, in 1784, the Montgolfier brothers demonstrated the world's first hot-air balloon in France. Just two years later, James Tytler made the first British ascent, and in the succeeding years there was something approaching balloon mania.

Demonstrations of ballooning attracted the crowds, and the daring aeronauts improved the spectacle by flying flags and streamers and letting off fireworks as they rose to the skies. But over time, as other forms of air transport developed, including powered aircraft, interest in ballooning died away. By the middle of the 20th century only a very few individuals, even among those interested in flight, remained aware of and taken with the idea of ballooning. One of those individuals was Don Cameron.

As a boy, Cameron made model aircraft, then moved on to gliders, and when he went to university to study aeronautical engineering he joined the university air squadron. It was over drinks at his local gliding club that he picked up a copy of *National Geographic* magazine. In it was an article about an American called Ed Yost, who had become interested in ballooning but realised that if it were ever to become popular again it would need to be modernised. So Yost set about designing a balloon appropriate for the 20th century. He made two vital changes to how they had been made previously. In the past, the balloon envelopes had usually been made out of expensive material such as silk, but Yost used modern, light, strong synthetics. In addition, the old hot-air balloons had required a furnace under the balloon that had to be stoked with fuel, but Yost's new version used propane cylinders attached to the burners. Aftrer reading the article, Cameron turned to a friend and said: 'We ought to make one of those.' And he did just that, working in his basement flat in Bristol,

and in 1967 his first balloon, *Bristol Belle*, was flown. He went on to make more balloons, and as interest grew and demand for them developed, he turned what had started as a hobby into a full-time business, and Cameron Balloons was born.

The factory is a rather nondescript industrial building tucked away down a South Bristol side street, but there is nothing nondescript about what goes on inside. The one thing you need in a balloon factory is a lot of open space, and with a floor area of 42,000 square feet (3,900 square metres), this building has it. By far the largest component in any balloon is the fabric that makes up the envelope. The material that is used varies in width from 1 to 1½ metres, and even a small balloon uses around a kilometre of fabric. But Cameron's company is currently constructing a giant. The Russian adventurer Fedor Konyukhov has already established a world record for a solo balloon flight around the world in just over 11 days. Now he has set his sights on creating a new world record for

← Assembling the burner that heats the air.

→ Installing the burner.

↙ Don Cameron and his first balloon, the Bristol Belle.

PREVIOUS PAGES Hannah Cameron checking the interior of a balloon that has been partially inflated inside the factory.

the highest flight by a hot-air balloon, which means that he will have to ascend above the current record height of 21,012.7 metres (68,939 feet). The very obvious problem is that as you get higher the air gets thinner, but in order for the balloon to keep on rising, the air density in it has to be lower than that of the outside atmosphere. And the only way to achieve that is to go big – so this balloon will be constructed using an astonishing 18 kilometres of fabric.

Everything here is on a huge scale. The fabric for the envelope is sewn on the top floor of the building in one big, open room. In garment factories, there are row upon row of workers sitting at their sewing machines. Here, by contrast, there are just a few, widely scattered to allow the space for the fabric. These are all highly skilled workers, for the whole integrity of the finished balloon depends on the quality of the stitching that holds the seams together. On the normal balloon, three types of material are used. The section at the top, where the hot air rises, has to be thicker than that for the central section, and the bottom part, nearest the burner, is made of flame-resistant material – the type

used for the seats in Formula 1 cars. The bottom of the balloon is open, and there is a valve at the top that is self-sealing but can be opened by the pilot to allow hot air to escape and the balloon to descend. On the outside, strong straps are attached that provide the support for the gondola, the part in which the pilot and any passengers travel.

Once it has been completed, the envelope is taken down to the next floor, where it is tested. It is laid out, occupying virtually the whole length of the room, and a heater is wheeled in to blow hot air to inflate it. It is a remarkable sight, seeing the fabric swell, slowly rising to the ceiling until it looks like a gigantic, if colourful, whale. This provides an opportunity for the staff to inspect both the outside and the inside of the envelope. This is not the only activity that goes on on this floor. During our visit, work was being done on artwork that a client had wanted to use to embellish his balloon.

On the ground floor a wide range of activities take place. It is here that the design team comes up with the exact specifications. The company produces a number of standard balloons as well

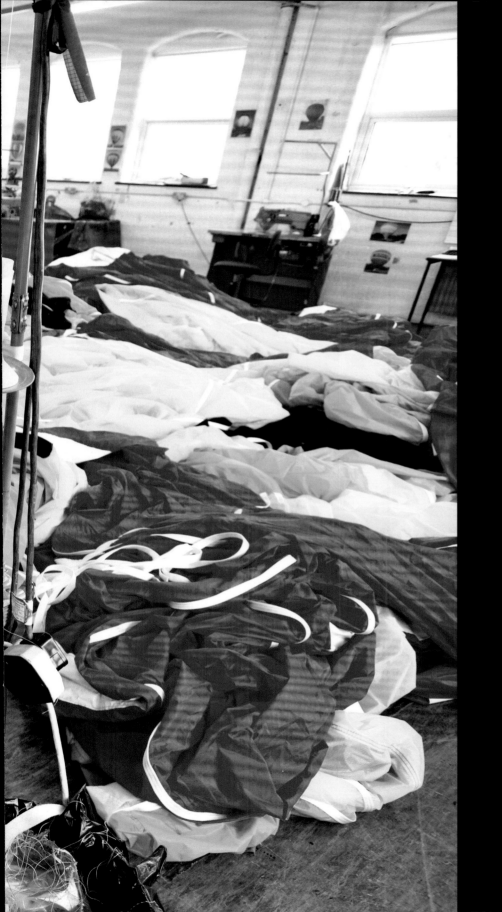

← The sewing room,
where strips of materia[l]
are sewn to create the
envelope.

as balloons for record-setting attempts, but there are often also very challenging demands for specialist and bizarre shapes to advertise customers' wares. Among the first specialist balloons they built was one in the form of a pair of jeans, but over the years they have got ever more elaborate. I remember being at a balloon festival and seeing what appeared to be a huge fire extinguisher flying over my head, but even that was surpassed by a remarkably realistic Jaguar car. Don Cameron explained that they could recreate most objects as long as they have bulk – though he would find

↑ Attaching the load straps that will carry the weight of the basket and its occupants.

↑ The seat for a one-man balloon.

a bicycle a pretty impossible request. It is, of course, not simply a matter of reproducing a given shape: the finished balloon must be balanced and aerodynamically sound. But the company's main activity is producing rather more conventional hot-air and gas-filled balloons, and the business is thriving: these days they turn out around a hundred balloons a year, the majority of which are exported to customers all round the world.

A long cutting table occupies another section, and there is a much smaller area where burners are assembled. The gondolas are made outside to Cameron's specifications. They are nearly all wickerwork baskets of various sizes. The exception is the arrangement for the one-man balloon, which is simply a seat, with attached controls for the burner and vent. Flying like this must be an interesting experience.

Once everything is completed, the envelope can be stuffed into a large bag for transporting, while the rest of the gear is carried in the gondola. The balloon is then ready to fly. In recent years, balloon festivals have attracted large crowds and, appropriately, the one held in Bristol each year is the grandest in the country. It is one thing to sit on the ground and admire the spectacle, but nothing quite matches the pleasure of actually flying. My first flight took place many years ago, with just myself and the pilot in the gondola. The first surprise is how quickly the balloon rises once released. Then, once you have reached an appropriate height, the wind wafts you gently across the land, literally giving you a bird's-eye view. When the burner's not actually lit it appears to be completely silent, but it isn't. Apparently the pilot light emits a high-pitched note that we can't hear, but dogs beneath the flight path can and they set up a furious, bewildered barking at the strange intruder above them. When eventually it is time to come back to earth it is just a case of finding a suitable piece of land, and then comes the touchdown, which, with a small balloon, usually involves the gondola tipping over and the pilot and passenger ending in a heap at the bottom of the basket. Flying in a balloon is an experience not to be forgotten – and it is one most of us are always happy to repeat. And whenever we do, we will almost certainly be taking off in a balloon manufactured by Cameron of Bristol.

↓ Testing one of the balloons shown overleaf for airworthiness.

FOOD AND DRINK

THE FIELD BARNS

If you drive into Swaledale in the northern part of the Yorkshire Dales and you come to the valley by crossing the hills, then you will look down on an extraordinary and unique landscape. In front of you, on the broad valley floor, is a chequerboard of meadows, each one with what could be taken, from a distance, to be a small cottage, though they are in fact barns – field barns – or, to the locals, cow houses.

This is clearly a farming landscape, but it is not the kind of landscape that one might find further south, for there is no farmhouse with its accompanying farmyard and barns. There are just, it seems, these isolated fields. The reason for this lies to a very large extent in the history of this region, which, until well into the 19th century, was dominated by lead mining. The village of Muker was a mining village, but the pay was desperately poor and most families supplemented their incomes by having a small patch of land on which to keep livestock. When the lead industry died, the people had to turn to the only other viable income in this area: they became farmers and acquired larger parcels of land, and the old miners' cottages, often enlarged, became farmhouses. They were still situated in the heart of the village, though, and the result is the unique farming system we see today.

William Raw took over Lane Farm in Muker from his parents, and the farmhouse where he and his wife, Carol, now live shows all the signs of probably having been built sometime in the 18th century, though it has greatly changed over the years: what is now an internal stone staircase, for instance, once stood against an outside wall. It is a short walk from the house, up a village lane, to reach the meadows. Here, William owns seven fields, scattered across the valley floor, five of which have barns in them. Come here in late May or June and the meadows are ablaze with colour. Predominating is the bright yellow of the buttercups, the yellow rattle and the globeflowers, but these meadows carry a wealth of other wildflowers: Carol Raw went for a

The summer visitors probably never see farm animals, but William has a herd of 15 beef cattle, though he once had rather more, and a flock of Swaledale sheep. In summer they are out on the upper pastures, among the rough grasses of the hillsides that close in the valley, so the best time to start the story is in winter. Crossing the fields, one reaches the first of the barns, close against the hillside. It is a simple structure, built out of locally gathered rough stones, just as the field walls have been. Rows of stones protrude at different heights from the wall, and William calls these 'troughs', but they serve exactly the same purpose as the 'throughs' of a drystone wall – they bind the whole structure together. Inside are some of the cattle; originally they would have been tied up in stalls, but now they are free to move about, and have room to do so. A wooden ladder leads up to the hayloft, and from here William can easily drop the feed down to the cattle. Everything is organised for efficiency. Round

walk one day and counted twenty different species, but she certainly didn't see them all. Wood cranesbill is an easily spotted resident with its attractive bluish-violet flowers, and other regulars include pignut and lady's mantle – together with the less welcome, at least as far as the farmers are concerned, melancholy thistle. The meadows attract a large number of visitors, and because this has been designated an Area of Special Scientific Interest (ASSI), they are carefully protected. The national park authority has laid a pathway of stone slabs across the meadows and installed gated stiles in the drystone walls that mark the boundaries. On a sunny day, the path can seem as busy as a town centre pavement, with walkers admiring the beauty of the scenery. Yet how many realise that the flowering meadows only exist because of those barns that they might walk past without a second glance? What we are actually seeing is a splendid ecologically sound system that was developed before the word 'ecology' had even been formed.

↑ Scattering fresh straw on the barn floor.

↓→ Feeding the cattle.

PREVIOUS PAGES
William Raw with his sheepdog Floss beside one of his Swaledale field barns.

← Looking down into the barn from the hay loft.

the back of the barn is an opening high in the wall. The ground is higher here, the barn being tight up against the hillside, making it easier to pitch hay up into the loft from here.

Twice a day in winter, regardless of the weather, William visits his barns, making sure there is plenty of fodder and taking the cattle out for a drink from the trough at the end of a barn, improvised out of an old bath tub. He regularly has to clean out the solid muck – the urine drains away via a gully on the barn floor. The muck is piled up behind a stone slab that prevents it from sliding down the slope, and it is a vital part of the whole system, becoming a rich natural manure which, once the winter snows have gone, will be spread out on the meadow to nourish the fields. Immediately after the Second World War, the government encouraged the Dales farmers to be 'more efficient' – that is, they should spray the meadows to get rid of 'the weeds'(ie the flowers), and spread artificial fertiliser. Today that policy has been reversed. No artificial fertilisers are used and grants are paid to maintain the more natural system. In part this is due to a desire to protect what most people would regard as a landscape of great natural beauty, and it is also a recognition that in an area that now offers very limited job opportunities, tourism is important and the meadows bring in walkers and other visitors. There was official recognition of what William does in 2012, when, coinciding with the Queen's 60 years on the throne, a scheme was put forward to recognise fine meadows in every county of England. Prince Charles came here, and three of William's meadows are officially Coronation Meadows – and the Raw family have a plaque to prove it. It is fair to say that without grants, the system would be unsustainable. This method of farming requires a lot of physical work, but for William, this is what he has done all his working life.

'I'm old-fashioned,' he says, 'and I'm not going to change now.'

As spring appears and the grass begins to grow, William and his working dog Floss go up to the high pasture to bring down the sheep. Swaledales are a hardy breed and the ewes give birth out in the open, but the lambs get a chance to romp in the new grass and nibble it before being returned to the hillsides. The cattle, too, get to graze briefly before they return to the high pastures as well. Then the meadows are left alone and the flowers begin to rise up through the grasses. By the middle of July, they will have seeded to produce next year's crop and the meadows can be cut and the hay taken to the barns ready for next winter. The circle of the year is complete.

↖ The Coronation Meadows in early June – crane bill and pignut can be seen among the meadow buttercups.

← Autumn in Swaledale.

↗ William Raw's barns and Coronation Meadows in winter.

→ Watering the cattle.

OVERLEAF The view down Swaledale – there are at least 29 barns visible here.

PORK PIES

This is not about pork pies in general but about one very specific and famous variety – the Melton Mowbray pork pie. This pie has two seemingly unlikely origins – the making of Stilton cheese and the hunting of foxes.

The Inclosure Acts of the 17th and 18th centuries brought a lot of what had once been common land into private ownership. It made for more efficient agriculture and in particular a huge increase in good pasture, from which there followed a much greater supply of milk. The surplus could be used to make cheese, and the local speciality was Stilton, much of it made then as now in Melton Mowbray. The whey not used for the cheese was fed to fatten the local pigs. This was also a great area for fox hunting – and huntsmen wanted something tasty to put in their saddlebags when out for the day. The local bakers hit on the bright idea of using the large quantities of pork available by cooking it and wrapping it in pastry – the pork pie was born. But it was thanks to a lady called Mary Dickinson that the very special Melton Mowbray pie began to emerge. Her grandson, John Dickinson, bought a bakery in the town in 1851. He was later joined by Joseph Morris, and there is still a business called Dickinson and Morris making pies on exactly the same site to this day.

The actual bakery is right behind the shop, and is every bit as busy, turning out 4,000 pies a week. That seems a lot, but in the six days leading up to Christmas the output rises to a colossal 30,000. Obviously these are very special pies, and their uniqueness is recognised in law. After years of legal argument, the Melton Mowbray pie was awarded protected status under European law, which means that the pies not only have to be made in a specified geographical area with Melton Mowbray at its heart, but they also have to conform to special rules, which include only using uncured pork – no bacon or ham – and putting in no additives other than seasoning. We were given a demonstration of traditional pie making by Master Pork Pie Baker and Managing Director Stephen Hallam.

The first step is making the pastry. This is hot-water pastry made with flour, water and lard, which is basically pork fat. Once made, the pastry is allowed to rest and is brought out for use the next day and raised to room temperature. A pork pie is 50% meat and 50% crust, so the correct amount of pastry is selected for each pie. Some is set aside for the lid and the rest is formed into a disc. A wooden dolly is then placed in the centre of the disc and the pastry is pulled up the side (*see photograph below*). Once the pastry has reached the top of the cylinder, the dolly

is removed. The pie is then filled with the meat, which is finely chopped pork shoulder. The lid is added and attached to the sides, then crimped by pressing with the fingers. The crust is lightly glazed with beaten egg and the pie is now ready for the oven, where it will join the rest of the batch and stay for an hour and a half. There is one other ingredient to add – jelly. This is created by heating pigs' trotters. Once the pies are cooked, two holes are made at the top; jelly is poured into one and the air escapes from the other. During this whole process, the pie will have settled slightly, giving it the distinctive bow-sided appearance.

There is no question about it – the pies look delectable. But what matters is the flavour, not the appearance. As soon as you bite in, the first thing you notice is the crumbly, tasty crust. It has such a good flavour and texture that you could eat it on its own as a biscuit. Then you get to the meat, and it seems clear that its quality is partly the reason for the intense flavour; another reason is the lack of additives, apart from the company's own seasoning – and it's not letting on exactly what that is. This is a pie that deserves to be listed, along with its neighbour, Stilton cheese, and such illustrious foreign products as champagne, as being special and worthy of preservation. Its success also, perhaps, shows that when you have been making something successfully for over a century and a half, there's not much point in changing the recipe.

SALMON FISHING

Most people will think of salmon fishing as involving rod and fly on a very expensive reach of a suitable river. But there is another tradition of fishing that doesn't involve privately owned stretches of rivers, nor are rods used. This is net fishing in estuaries, and no one knows how long it has been practised.

Today, there are two places where this type of fishing is still carried out, the Solway Firth and the River Severn. There is a clue to the antiquity of fishing in these two regions, each of which has its own unique style, though operating on very similar principles. That clue is in the name used on the Solway – haaf net fishing. 'Haaf' is the Norse word for 'channel', and it is generally believed that it was the Vikings who first introduced this type of fishing to Britain. Fishing on the Severn is known as lave net fishing, and although there are no records of when it was started, it has certainly been practised for many centuries. And it is still practised today in exactly the same way that it always has been.

The River Severn has the second highest tidal range in the world, just beaten by the Bay of Fundy on Canada's Atlantic coast. This means that at low spring tides it is possible to wade far out from the shore, though this is certainly not something the inexperienced should try for themselves. The lave fishermen have been doing this for generations and have an intimate knowledge of the river, and they even have their own names for particular spots that to the uninitiated look exactly the same as every other bit of river. Today fishing is carried out from Black Rock under the shadow of the second Severn Bridge. The nets have remained unchanged in their method of construction. They are generally made by the fishermen themselves using entirely traditional methods – what distinguishes these nets from others is the frames to which they are attached. These are Y-shaped, with the two arms, known as the rimes, being made of willow. The net is loosely slung between them. They are hinged to the handle, the hand-staff being made of oak. The men wade out into the water with the nets across their shoulders, with the rimes folded against the head-staffs. Once in position, the net is opened out and spread by another piece of the equipment – the headboard. Each fisherman holds the net in front of his body, facing into the running tide. One hand is on the hand-staff and the other is beneath the water, holding the headboard. He entwines his fingers in the netting so that he can sense the moment a fish enters the net. At that point he must smartly lift the hand-staff to bring the net clear of the water and slide down the headboard to close the net and keep the salmon trapped. There are basically two methods of fishing: one is to pick a spot and wait patiently for a salmon to swim in; the other is to be more active and look for any telltale movement in the water that indicates a fish on the move. Then the net has to be quickly deployed before the fish reaches deep water.

The fishing season is short, running from June to August, and this is certainly not an occupation for anyone wanting commercial success. Halfway through the 2017 season a grand total of three salmon had been landed.

↓ When fishing begins the nets are submerged beneath the surface.

As one of the fishermen wryly remarked, they had seen a seal in the estuary that was getting more fish than they were. The men of the Black Rock fishery carry on because they value the tradition that their families have followed for many generations. One would have thought that, given the small size of their catch, these fishermen were scarcely a threat to fish stocks, yet until recently there was a very real possibility that new regulations would bring this pastime to a halt. A rule was proposed that all the salmon caught had to be released; but as

they were unlikely to survive being netted this seemed unnecessary, and certainly you would have to be truly dedicated to spend hours up to your waist in cold water only to have to put back whatever you did catch for it then to die. Fortunately, however, the Welsh Assembly took the sensible view that this form of fishing was a tradition worth preserving, and in 2017 the fishermen were granted a renewed licence with no conditions attached. So lave net fishing is set to continue for a few more years at least.

↑ The net fully extended and ready for use.

↗→ Boating out to catch the tide *(top right)*; preparing to set up a net *(middle)*; taking out the nets ready to start fishing *(bottom)*.

PREVIOUS PAGES Lave net fishermen heading out into the River Severn.

↑ The men make their own nets from locally sourced wood.

→ Hoping for a catch.

↓ Weaving the net.

STARGAZY PIE

On 23 December, the Cornish fishing village of Mousehole celebrates the achievements of Tom Bawcock. This seems to be a very old tradition, but no one seems to be clear on exactly how old, nor on precisely what is being celebrated.

One version has it that it was traditional to eat a variety of fish at Christmas, but Tom was lazy and hadn't supplied the necessary amount or selection, so his wife sent him out to catch more just before Christmas to avoid shaming her as the only wife in the village who couldn't produce a splendid array of fish. The most popular version has him instead as the hero of an event in the 16th century, in a year when there had been such a harsh winter that none of the boats had been able to get out to sea and the villagers were close to starvation. Tom

braved the storms on his own and came back with seven different types of fish. They were baked into a pie, and to show that there really were fish in it, the heads were stuck out from the top of the pastry. As the fish were all apparently looking up to the sky, it became known as stargazy pie, and it is prepared on 23 December every year to celebrate the occasion. There is even a traditional poem celebrating the event. Here is the first verse; the spelling might seem odd, but if you say it out loud – preferably in a Cornish accent – it makes sense:

A merry plaas you may believe
Was Mowsel pon Tom Bawcock's Eve
To be theer then oo wudn wesh
To sup o sidam sorts o fish

The practice of supplying seven different types of fish was later abandoned in favour of using only pilchards. This was reasonable, as for many years pilchard fishing was the main activity of not just Mousehole but the majority of Cornish fishing ports. There is a reminder of those days in the 'Huer's Hut' that stands on the cliffs near Newquay. Looking down into the sea, the huer could see the shoals of fish and direct the boats to the right spot to catch them.

Tom Bawcock's Eve is a big event in Mousehole, and it has been embellished in recent years by hanging lights all round the harbour, with a lantern procession winding through the village. It culminates in the arrival of the stargazy pie, carried into the Ship Inn by a local dressed as Tom and then paraded around. Apparently these days his reward is 25 pints of Guinness – all to be drunk on the day. Clearly life in Mousehole is becoming a little more sober these days, as it used to be 30! But the pie itself remains unchanged, with seven different fish inspecting the heavens.

← The heads poking up through the crust give the pie its name.

→ A stargazy pie being presented at the Ship Inn, Mousehole.

THE SWEET SHOP

If you are of a certain age, there are certain words that instantly bring back memories of childhood, and among them are the names of sweets that you used to eat – and that you probably thought had vanished from the shelves forever.

Everyone probably has their own list, but here are a few that most will recognise: bulls eyes, pear drops, aniseed balls, liquorice torpedoes and perhaps the best known of all, the humbug. Well, they may not be available everywhere, but you can get them all in the world's oldest sweet shop, in Pateley Bridge, Yorkshire.

The old market town climbs steeply up from the bridge across the River Nidd, its high street flanked by reassuringly solid buildings, many built from great blocks of sandstone. Turn off this road at any point and you are liable to find yourself in an odd little cobbled alley of great charm, and there, very near the top, opposite a butcher's offering such rare delicacies as a black pudding and apple pie, is the 'Oldest Sweet Shop in England'. The sign is unusually modest for Yorkshire: it is in fact, officially, the oldest sweet shop in the world. The building itself is certainly old, with the date of 1661 inscribed on the lintel of the front door, and it was usual practice in this part of the world to carve the date as soon as the building was completed. Not a lot appears to be known about its early history, but there is some evidence that it has seen several alterations over the centuries. It occupies a corner site, and the side wall seems to have once had a window that was later blocked in. What we do know is that it was first used as a sweet shop in 1827 and has been ever since.

The shop was really something very novel when it opened. Sugar had been a luxury commodity in the 18th century, but the introduction of mechanisation on the plantations and processing plants had brought down the price to the point where it could be made into comparatively cheap sweets. The other great innovation came a little later, in 1847, when Joseph Fry of Bristol discovered a way of turning chocolate into a paste that could be pressed into bars. These were the two main types of confectionery sold – sweets made by boiling sugar, and chocolate and chocolate bars. They still are.

Enter the shop and its age is immediately apparent in the low ceilings and exposed beams. The sense of walking into the past is enhanced by everything else in there.

The most striking features are the rows of shelves behind the counter packed with glass jars containing every conceivable variety of colourful boiled sweets. Even the till is an old-fashioned, highly decorated machine with keys a bit like a typewriter, and the scales are the old style made by Avery, with a metal pan and a pointer running over the scale above it. The present owners, Keith and Gloria Tordoff, obviously realise the value of nostalgia in attracting in the customers: it would be a strange child who wouldn't want to know what was in all those jars, and where parents might be prepared to drag them past a modern confectionery shop, the appeal of the old draws them in. This is a place that is steeped in tradition, selling traditional goods in an equally traditional setting. And when Keith and Gloria retire, the next generation is all ready to step in and take over. There is, of course, one factor that will be essential for their continued success – the existence of equally traditional suppliers, sweet manufacturers still producing sweets using the technology that was around when the shop first opened. Fortunately, such suppliers do still exist, so for the forseeable future at least, this sweet shop is safe.

→ A child's delight – row upon row of traditional sweets in glass jars in the world's oldest sweet shop.

THE
TRADITIONAL PUB

What exactly is a traditional pub? In the distant past there was a real distinction between inns, which primarily existed to accommodate guests and would serve them with food and drink, and alehouses, which were mainly, if not entirely, devoted to selling alcoholic beverages. The former were often very respectable places: Jane Austen's heroines were perfectly happy to go to the local inn for a dance, but they would never have set foot in the latter.

We get a notion of what a Tudor alehouse might have been like from Shakespeare's *Twelfth Night*, when Malvolio berates the boisterous Toby Belch and his friends for turning Olivia's peaceful home into an alehouse. Today, those differences have largely been forgotten, but new varieties have appeared in recent years, notably the gastro pub, which all too often appears to be a thinly disguised restaurant that will reluctantly serve you a pint, and where you can't sit down because the tables all have 'reserved' notices on them.

A traditional pub should be one that serves traditional fare – and that means real ales and ciders as the first priority, with food as an extra rather than the primary point of interest. It should also be a place where there is flexibility – the good pub is essentially a social institution. It is one of the few places in Britain where total strangers don't feel uncomfortable talking to each other. Many pubs are housed in old buildings, creating an atmosphere of age. But there is no one pattern that covers them all: some favour exposed beams and inglenook fireplaces, where others are more cut glass and polished brass. In this section, Rob Scott and I have tried to choose a range of pubs that give an idea of the rich variety available, but we are all too aware that every pub enthusiast will have their own shortlist – and it will probably be entirely different from our selection.

wool trade, and every year there were two important wool fairs, where cloth was sold. The building was originally a wool store, but the many buyers who came to the fair were accommodated in what appears to have been a large dormitory on the topmost floor. Changes came over the years, and from its origins as a monastic hostelry it became a coaching inn on the main road from Bristol to Salisbury. No doubt it has seen many cheerful occasions – but it also had one less happy period. Following the failed Monmouth rebellion of 1685, Judge Jeffreys held court here as part of the Bloody Assizes. Twelve unfortunates were convicted and executed on the green outside the inn. Today the site has a much happier use – it is home to the local cricket club.

The building was originally bigger than it is today – part was demolished in the 17th century. The ground floor is part of the original building constructed in the 14th century, and one can see its antiquity in its solid stone construction, its mullioned windows and its handsome arched doorway. The two upper floors were largely remodelled

There are several contenders for title of oldest pub in Britain – many sticking a Ye Olde in front of their name to emphasise the point. The George Inn at Norton St Philip in Somerset is one that has quite a good claim, but that is not really why it has been selected. It has been chosen because of its essential character, wearing its years with dignity. Travellers coming across the pub might think they recognise its age by the timber framing on the jettied upper storeys, but they are in fact the 'modern' part of the building. Its origins go back further to the monks of the nearby priory at Hinton Charterhouse. Much of the wealth of the district and its priory came from the

↑ Birch Hall Inn at Beck Hole in the North Yorkshire Moors.

→ The cosy bar at the Birch Hall Inn.

PREVIOUS PAGES
The ornate interior of the pub still known as the Philharmonic Dining Rooms in Liverpool.

→ The little sweet shop tucked in between the bars at Birch Hall Inn.

in the 15th century, when it seems the building's role as an inn had overtaken its use as a wool store. The whole is topped by a magnificent stone slate roof – during restoration in 1988 it was stripped down to the supporting timbers, and it is a mark of the original craftsmanship that of the almost 30,000 tiles taken down, 70% were reused. This is a building that has seen many alterations over the years, but step inside and you are taken back through the centuries. As one might expect from a building that has seen so many changes through the years, it is difficult to make sense of the layout of the rooms, but everywhere there is the sense of antiquity, from the exposed timbers to the stone walls. So this is a building with a rich history – but that alone doesn't make a good pub. However, the George wears its history lightly and has never lost sight of its main function – to provide a friendly, warm atmosphere for the enjoyment of good ale and decent grub.

The George's historical importance and good location on a busy main road are obvious – but why on earth does the Tan Hill Inn exist at all? It is Britain's highest pub, at 1,732 feet above sea level, in a remote moorland setting near the northern edge of the Yorkshire Dales National Park, and it regularly gets snowed in during the winter months. Yet, although the present inn is rather later, built in the 17th century, there has been a pub on this site since at least the 16th century, when, even back then, it was recorded as being remote. The answer to

OVERLEAF The Tan Hill Inn sits within a desolate landscape.

→ The bar at Tan Hill Inn.

← The Drovers Inn at Inverarnan near the northern end of Loch Lomond.

↓ The ferocious stuffed bear that greets visitors to the Drovers.

be in this location. Inside is just as rugged, with stone-flagged floors, rough undressed stone walls and, of course, in the winter a fire burning bright. The pub offers local real ales and ciders and the sort of hearty pub grub you want if you've just walked several miles across open moorland. In its essentials it is much like many other pubs in the Dales, but its history and unique setting make it a very special place.

City pubs are, not surprisingly, generally quite unlike their country cousins – louder, brasher, altogether more ornate. Where a village might have just one or two pubs, the city pub can be surrounded by competitors, all demanding attention. So it is necessary for them to try and stand out from the crowd. The heyday of the city pub came in the years leading up to the First World War, when new pubs were a riot of polished brass and cut glass, but few were as ornate as the Philharmonic in Liverpool or, to give it its

this mystery is perhaps surprising: this was once the centre of a coal-mining region, with two busy collieries – the Tan Hill mine and the King's Pit mine. It was a busy spot, with kilns for converting much of the coal into coke, and a steam engine puffing away above a shaft. And where there are mines there is also a mining village, so the pub was once surrounded by cottages. The inn would have been the social centre for a whole community. But the final pit was closed in 1929, and with no work, there was no reason for anyone to go on living in such a bleak spot, so the cottages were abandoned and fell into ruin.

That should have been the end of the Tan Hill Inn, but by then the age of the motor car had dawned, and the idea of visiting the highest pub in Britain in a wild setting had a romantic appeal. Those, however, were the days when drink-driving laws were less strict and less enforceable than they are today – to get arrested back then, you probably had to be rolling drunk, and there was no breathalyser. With greater enforcement, remote country pubs became less popular. But circumstances seemed always to favour this old place: in 1965, Britain's first National Trail, the Pennine Way, was opened and it runs right past the pub. This hugely popular

long-distance walk brought a steady stream of walkers to the door looking for food, a drink and, in some cases, somewhere to stay the night. As a result, the pub did not just survive, it was extended, but in the process has never lost its robust character. It remains what it has always been, a sturdy no-nonsense stone building, as it needs to

↑ Part of the menagerie of stuffed beasts in the hallway of the Drovers.

full title, The Philharmonic Dining Rooms. It takes its name from the nearby Philharmonic Hall, which is a little confusing as the latter is clearly a far more modern building, but that is only because it has replaced the original, built in the 1840s.

The pub was built in the last decade of the 19th century and designed by Liverpool architect Walter W Thomas. This was a time when Art Nouveau was *the* fashionable style of the day, and there are few finer examples than the ornate entrance to the building, which was designed by the local architect

H Bloomfield Bare, who also ran an Arts and Crafts studio at Port Sunlight. It is a riot of twisted forms, and over the door is the motto *Pacem Amo* – Peace and Love. It might seem that nothing inside could match such an exuberant entrance, but the job of designing the interior went to students at the School of Applied Art at Liverpool University, who gave it their all. The curved bar stands in the centre of the first room, where there is

a profusion of detail. The walls are panelled in wood, the floor is covered in mosaic tiles and the roof features elaborate plasterwork. Famous worthies of the day look out at you from either side of the fireplace: the heroes of the Boer War, Lord Baden-Powell and Field Marshal Earl Roberts. Customer comfort is assured by the fine leather upholstery. Other rooms branch off from here, the first two suitably named after the most admired composers of the late 19th century, Brahms and Liszt – and rather too appropriately juxtaposed for a pub perhaps.

The finest room of all is the Grande Saloon – so grand in fact it almost earns that rather pompous final 'e'. The walls are decorated with beaten copper panels depicting various fish and fowl. Caryatids lead up to an even more ornate ceiling with stained-glass roof lights, and there is more stained glass in the windows, one of which bears the message 'Music is the language of mankind'. A rather more prosaic motto appears on the immense cut-glass mirror over the mantelpiece, which quite properly shows the name of the pub, but also advertises gin. There is one other room that deserves a special mention: the gents is almost as grand as anywhere else in the building, featuring genuine marble. For anyone with a taste for Victorian extravagance, this is the pub to visit.

Many readers will have their own favourite pub, and all kinds of factors will have come together to make it seem attractive. Being in a great position and having a quirky individuality certainly help – and these are qualities that definitely

↑ The George at Norton St. Philip.

↘ The entrance to the George betrays its medieval origins.

apply to the Birch Hall Inn at Beck Hole near Goathland on the North Yorkshire Moors. No one is quite certain how long the building has been here but it is certainly a very long time, and a painting of some two centuries ago shows it as a thatched cottage – certainly not a grand hall. But in the 19th century the area changed dramatically when mining for iron ore and coal began, bringing with it a lot of thirsty miners. The house was extended and became an inn, with accommodation and a shop. Then mining came to an end and Beck Hole returned to peace and quiet, but the pub survived, serving locals and ever-increasing numbers of visiting walkers and tourists. However, its character has never changed, and amazingly it still has a shop, selling not essential foods, but sweets. This is sandwiched between the two bars. To one side is the Little Bar, once part of the original

shop, and to the other is, as you might expect, the Big Bar, though both are quite small. If you are in the Big Bar, then you have to order your beer through the hatch in the wall. It is, quite simply, a delight.

Scottish pubs tend to be rather different from either English or Welsh pubs and can be roughly divided into two categories – bars and inns. To a visitor at least it tends to be the latter that prove the more interesting. That is certainly true of the Drovers Inn at Inverarnan at the northern end of Loch Lomond. I first came here some years ago when it was an overnight stop as I walked the West Highland Way. It was certainly colourful but, to put it politely, a touch basic. You don't really expect to find your bed propped up on old milk crates. Well, it is still colourful, but the milk crates are certainly gone for good and it is a thriving pub anyone would be happy to find at the end of a long day's walk in the hills.

The outside is built of rather austere stone and dates back to the beginning of the 18th century. It stood on the drove road along which Highlanders used to bring their cattle to market. But there is nothing on the exterior to prepare you for what you are greeted by when you walk inside. Of all the things you

might expect to find there, a stuffed grizzly bear is probably not one of them. But he is not alone: a variety of other stuffed animals and birds decorate the walls, though they are species rather more likely to be found on Scottish hills. One animal not present, though described in some detail as part of the wall decoration, is the wild haggis – well, we ignorant English will believe anything. The Scottish theme continues throughout the pub – in everything from the tartan stair carpet to claymores and shields. This is the

↑ An upper room
at the George.

OVERLEAF The court-
yard at the George.

sort of thing that could be irritating in some circumstances, but here it is so gloriously over the top that it just makes you smile the moment you come in. But, as always, what matters is what you are served and how comfortable you feel – and the Drovers doesn't disappoint on either count. Come in winter and there's a warming fire, decent beer and a menu that offers traditional pub

grub, including, as one would expect, haggis, presumably caught locally. It is quite a feat to combine extravagant décor and ornaments with homely comfort, but somehow the Drovers manages to do just that: it is a place where anyone could drop in for a drink and perhaps a meal, but it is especially welcoming to anyone who has just spent a day on the hills and might well be arriving cold and wet, but certainly hungry and thirsty. This is exactly the sort of place all walkers hope to find at the end of their journey.

A FIERY FINALE

UP HELLY AA

Shetland has a spectacular annual event that both celebrates the end of the old year and looks forward to the new. In its present form the festival of Up Helly Aa only dates back to the 1880s, but it seems to have its origins in earlier rather riotous events when barrels of burning tar were rolled through the streets of Lerwick towards the end of January. This gave way to the rather less hazardous notion of a torchlight procession. Then it was decided to use the occasion to celebrate the islands' Viking past.

The Vikings have a reputation as raiders and pillagers, but they also came as settlers. They first arrived in these northern islands around AD 800 and not only made them their home, but incorporated Shetland and Orkney into the Norse kingdom. The islands remained Norse until the 15th century, at which point the rather impoverished Danes were unable to raise the money for a dowry for their Princess Margaret, who was to marry James III of Scotland, so they mortgaged Orkney and Shetland as a temporary measure in 1468. But having acquired the islands, the Scots decided to keep them and Shetland was officially annexed in 1471. The years of Norse rule were over but never forgotten. And nowhere is the Norse tradition celebrated more spectacularly than in Lerwick on the last Tuesday of January.

The festival today is a huge event not just for Shetland but for visitors who come to see the spectacle – and huge events like this require equally huge amounts of work and preparation. The participants, in Viking costumes, are divided into groups with, at their heart, the Jarl Squad led by the Guizer Jarl. He is a resplendent figure with winged helmet and armour, and armed with an axe. The main items of costume are passed on from year to year, but each year he chooses his own motif and colour scheme for his cloak and kirtle. The Jarl Squad have to make their own costumes, a process that begins two years in advance. They also have to decide on a motif and colour scheme for their shields.

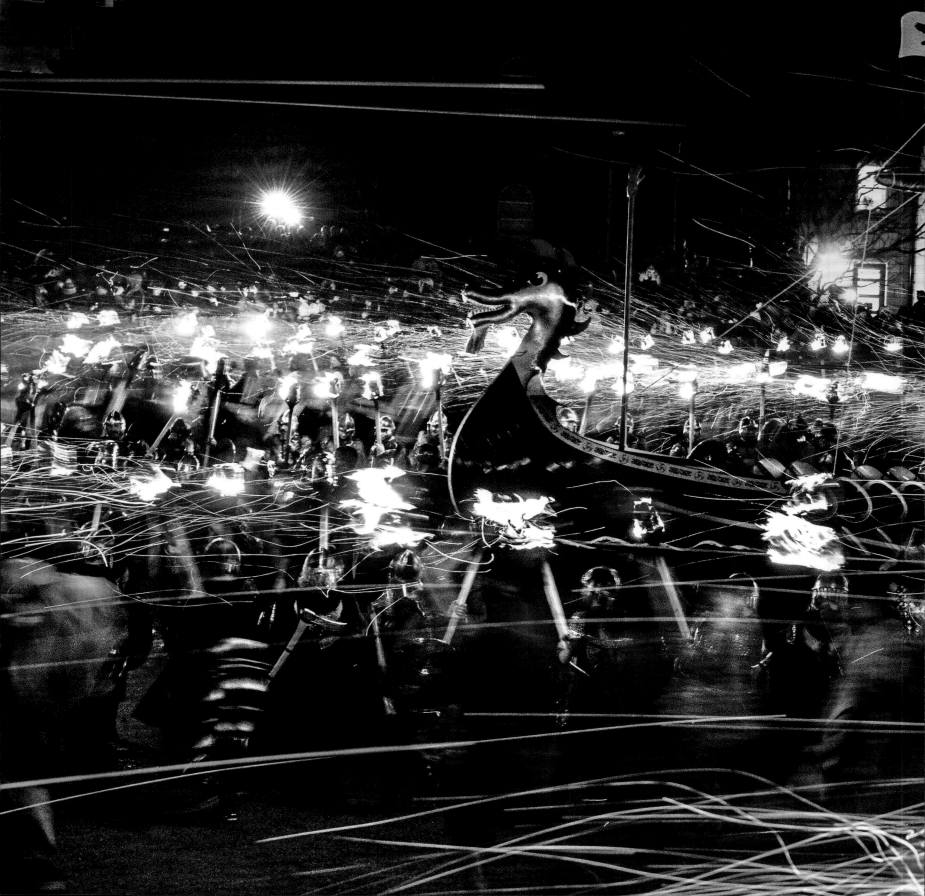

At the heart of the whole ceremony is a replica of a Viking longship. This is no mere model, but a robust vessel 9.2 metres long, 1.8 metres across the beam and with a 6-metre-high mast. At the front is the magnificent dragon's-head prow. Like the costumes, this has to be made afresh every year by local craftsmen – and the Guizer Jarl has the honour of choosing the paint scheme for the vessel. Preparing for Up Helly Aa really does involve the whole community. It is a vast amount of effort to put in for an event that will last for just one day – but what a memorable day that is.

Throughout the day there are processions through the town, not to mention a certain amount of feasting, but the great spectacle comes at night time. One thousand flares are prepared, soaked in fuel and handed out to the Viking warriors. The Guizer Jarl and the galley pass through the ranks, and at 7.30 in the evening a maroon is set off as the signal for the torches to be lit. Now the whole procession moves off through the crowds of spectators in a scene that really does seem to carry you back in time to an age before streets were even lit by gas lamps, let alone electricity. It is spectacular, the air full of the glare of torches and flying sparks. The climax of the ceremony comes at the playing field where the Jarls gather to hurl their torches into the galley as in a traditional Viking funeral pyre. But in this ceremony it is the old year that is being burned away – not a Norse chieftain. A year's work vanishes in flames – and it is time to start all over again, preparing for next year.

Up Helly Aa may be a Victorian invention, but it looks and feels like an ancient tradition with its roots in the pagan past – and it also looks like a tradition that will last for many generations to come.

THE SITES

A MARITIME NATION

THE SHIPWRIGHT
Stirling & Son, Crapstone Barton,
Buckland Monachorum, Devon
PL20 7LG
● www.stirlingandson.co.uk

THE ROPE WORKS
Master Ropemakers, The Historic
Dockyard, Chatham, Kent ME4 4TG
● www.master-ropemakers.co.uk

THE BARGE MATCH
Information on matches from:
● www.associationofbargemen.org.uk

PS WAVERLEY
Waverley Excursions Ltd., Waverley
Steam Navigation Co. Ltd., 36
Lancefield Quay, Glasgow G3 8HA
● www.waverleyexcursions.co.uk

ON THE MOVE

THE WHEELWRIGHT AND COACH BUILDER
Mike Rowland & Son, No.1 Wheelers
Yard, Colyton, Devon EX24 6DT
● www.wheelwright.org.uk

THE HORSE TRAM
Douglas Bay Horse Tramway,
Strathallan Crescent, Douglas
IM1 4NR

THE STEAM RAILWAY
Isle of Man Steam Railway,
Steam Railway Station, Banks
Crescent, Douglas IM1 5PT

THE ELECTRIC TRAM
Manx Electric Railway, Derby
Castle, Douglas IM2 4NR
For information on all Isle of
Man transport systems visit:
● www.visitisleofman.com

FAIRS AND ENTERTAINMENTS

APPLEBY HORSE FAIR
Information on:
● www.applebyfair.org

THE FAIRGROUND ORGAN
Dean Organ Builders, The Music
Box Shop, 38–40 Bristol Road,
Whitchurch, Nr. Bristol BS14 0PT
● www.deanorganbuilders.co.uk

THE CIRCUS
Information on:
● www.giffordscircus.com

PUNCH AND JUDY
Poulton's Punch and Judy,
information on:
● www.poultonpuppets.co.uk

THE THEATRE
Tyne Theatre and Opera House,
117 Westgate Road, Newcastle-
upon-Tyne NE1 4AG
● www.tynetheatreandoperahouse.uk

UP AND OVER

NEWCASTLE SWING BRIDGE
Swing Bridge, Newcastle,
Tyne and Wear NE1 3RG
● www.newcastlegateshead.com/
things-to-do/swing-bridge-p562331

NEWPORT TRANSPORTER BRIDGE
Visitor centre, Transporter Bridge,
Brunel Street, Newport NP20 2JY
www.newport.gov.uk/heritage/
transporter-bridge

SALTBURN CLIFF LIFT
Cliff Lift, Saltburn by the Sea
● www.saltburnbysea.com/html/
clifflift.html

FABRICS

RUSH MATTING
Rushmatters, Grange Farm,
Colesden, Bedfordshire MK44 2DB
● www.rushmatters.co.uk

THE HORSEHAIR MILL
John Boyd Textiles Ltd., Higher Flax
Mills, Castle Cary, Somerset BA7 7DY
● www.johnboydtextiles.co.uk

THE LACE MAKERS
GH Hurt & Son, 65 High Road,
Chilwell, Nottingham NG9 4AJ
● www.ghhurt.com

HARRIS TWEED
The Harris Tweed Authority,
The Town Hall, 2 Cromwell Street,
Stornoway, Isle of Lewis HS1 2DB
● www.harristweed.org

SPORTS AND GAMES

THE FOOTBALL MATCH
Ashbourne football, information on:
● www.visitpeakdistrict.com/
whatson/royal-shrovetide-football

REAL TENNIS
Jesmond Dene Real tennis Club,
Matthew Bank, Newcastle-
upon-Tyne NE2 3RE
● www.jdrtc.co.uk

THE HIGHLAND GAMES
Information from Scottish
Highland Games Association:
● www.shga.co.uk

BALLOONS
Cameron Balloons, St. Johns Street,
Bedminster, Bristol BS3 4NH
● www.cameronballoons.co.uk

FOOD AND DRINK

THE FIELD BARNS
Yorkshire Dales Millennium Trust,
Clapham, North Yorkshire LA2 8DP
● www.ydmt.org

PORK PIES
Dickinson & Morris, Ye Olde Pork Pie
Shoppe, 10 Nottingham Street,
Melton Mowbray, Leicestershire
LE13 1NW ● www.porkpie.co.uk

SALMON FISHING
The Black Rock Lave Net Heritage
Fishery, Black Rock Road, Portskewett,
Monmouthshire NP26 5TP
● www.blackrocklavenets.co.uk

STARGAZY PIE
The Ship Inn, South Cliff,
Mousehole, Cornwall TR19 6QX
● www.shipinnmousehole.co.uk

THE SWEET SHOP
The Oldest Sweet Shop, 39 High Street,
Pateley Bridge, North Yorkshire HG3 5JZ
● www.oldestsweetshop.co.uk

TRADITIONAL PUBS
The George Inn, High Street,
Norton St. Philip, Somerset BA2 7LH
● www.georgeinnnsp.co.uk
Tan Hill Inn, Wreeth, Richmond,
Swaledale DL11 6ED
● www.tanhillinn.com
Birch Hall Inn, Beck Hole, Whitby, North
Yorkshire YO22 5LE www.beckhole.info
Philharmonic Dining Rooms,
36 Hope Street, Liverpool L1 9BX
● www.nicholsonspubs.co.uk/
restaurants/northwest/thephilharmonic
diningroomsliverpool
The Drovers Inn, Inverarnan,
Arrochar, Argyll & Bute G83 7DX
● www.droversinn.co.uk

A FIERY FINALE

Information at: ● www.uphellyaa.org

INDEX